REACHING FOR THE FUTURE
CREATIVE FINANCE FOR SMALLER COMMUNITIES

About the Urban Land Institute

The mission of the Urban Land Institute is to provide leadership in the responsible use of land and in creating and sustaining thriving communities worldwide. ULI is committed to

- Bringing together leaders from across the fields of real estate and land use policy to exchange best practices and serve community needs;
- Fostering collaboration within and beyond ULI's membership through mentoring, dialogue, and problem solving;
- Exploring issues of urbanization, conservation, regeneration, land use, capital formation, and sustainable development;
- Advancing land use policies and design practices that respect the uniqueness of both built and natural environments;
- Sharing knowledge through education, applied research, publishing, and electronic media; and
- Sustaining a diverse global network of local practice and advisory efforts that address current and future challenges.

Established in 1936, the Institute today has more than 37,000 members representing the entire spectrum of the land use and development disciplines. ULI relies heavily on the experience of its members. It is through member involvement and information resources that ULI has been able to set standards of excellence in development practice. The Institute has long been recognized as one of the world's most respected and widely quoted sources of objective information on urban planning, growth, and development.

Patrick L. Phillips
Global Chief Executive Officer, ULI

About the ULI Foundation

The mission of the ULI Foundation is to serve as the philanthropic source for the Urban Land Institute. The Foundation's programs raise endowment funds, major gifts, and annual fund monies to support the key initiatives and priorities of the Institute. Philanthropic gifts from ULI members and other funding sources help ensure ULI's future and its mission of providing leadership in the responsible use of land and in creating and sustaining thriving communities worldwide.

Recommended bibliographic listing:
McAvey, Maureen, Tom Murphy, and Bridget Lane. *Reaching for the Future: Creative Finance for Smaller Communities*. Washington, DC: Urban Land Institute, 2016.

ISBN: 978-0-87420-376-9

Urban Land Institute
1025 Thomas Jefferson St., NW
Suite 500 West
Washington, DC 20007-5201

Acknowledgments

City Contacts

A special thank you goes to the following people for their assistance in the development of the city case studies:

Skip Schwab
Vice President, East Liberty Development Initiative

Nancy Whitworth
Director, Economic Development, Greenville

James Harbaugh
City Center Lehigh Valley, Allentown

Michael Kowski
Development Services Department, Village of Orland Park

Anastasia Mileham
Vice President, Cincinnati Central City Development Corporation

Tori Torres
Johnson Development Corp., Sugar Land

Diane Williams
Partner, BDI (for assistance with Sugar Land)

Diane Barrett
Mayor's Office, Denver

Advisory Group

We are also grateful to the Advisory Group whose members offered insight and advice at the onset of this project:

Lisa Abuaf
Central City Manager
Portland, Oregon, Development Commission

Diane Barrett
Special Assistant to the Mayor
City and County of Denver

Lev Gershman
Managing Partner
Tideline Partners

James R. Harris
Partner
James R. Harris Partners LLC

Anne Haynes
Director of Transformative Development
MassDevelopment

Bert (Robert) Mathews III
Owner
The Mathews Company

Tommy Pacello
Project Manager, Neighborhood Economic Vitality
Mayor's Innovation Delivery Team, Memphis

Patrick Rhodes
Vice President of Development
Sora Development

Cassie Seagren
Deputy Chief of Staff, Mayor's Office
City of Omaha

Pamela Stein
Executive Director
ULI North Texas

Yaromir Steiner
Chief Executive Officer
Steiner + Associates

Karl Zavitkovsky
Economic Development Director
City of Dallas

About the Authors

Tom Murphy, ULI Canizaro/Klingbeil Families Chair for Urban Development, has been a senior resident fellow at the Urban Land Institute since 2006. He is the former mayor of Pittsburgh.

Maureen McAvey is the ULI Bucksbaum Family Chair for Retail. She has an extensive array of experience in public and private real estate development and land use positions.

Bridget Lane has been a frequent writer for ULI publications and is the director of Business Districts Inc. in Evanston, Illinois.

ULI Senior Executives

Patrick L. Phillips
Global Chief Executive Officer, and President, ULI Foundation

Michael Terseck
Chief Financial Officer/Chief Administrative Officer

Cheryl Cummins
Global Governance Officer

Lisette van Doorn
Chief Executive, ULI Europe

John Fitzgerald
Chief Executive, ULI Asia Pacific

Kathleen B. Carey
President and Chief Executive Officer, ULI Foundation

Lela Agnew
Executive Vice President, Strategic Communications

Marilee Utter
Executive Vice President, District Councils

Steve Ridd
Executive Vice President, Global Business Operations

About This Publication

This publication is inspired by the many communities that have taken the initiative to revitalize themselves and by the leaders who made it happen. We hope it will be used as a resource by communities that are aspiring to reach for the future.

Project Staff

Maureen McAvey
ULI Bucksbaum Family Chair for Retail

Tom Murphy
ULI Canizaro/Klingbeil Families Chair for Urban Development

Jess Zimbabwe
Ross Center for Public Leadership

Anita Kramer
Senior Vice President, Capital Markets

Alison Johnson
Program Manager, Content

Brett He
Arun Lertsumitkul
Amy Mulcahy
Interns, University of Sydney, New South Wales, Australia

Reema Singh
Intern, Carnegie Mellon University

James A. Mulligan
Senior Editor

Joanne Platt, Publications Professionals LLC
Manuscript Editor

Betsy Van Buskirk
Creative Director

Deanna Pineda, Muse Advertising Design
Book Designer

Craig Chapman
Senior Director, Publishing Operations

CONTENTS

Introduction

SOME CITIES ARE BREAKING THE RULES; exuding an appetite for risk, vision, and leadership; forming great partnerships; and shaping their communities for the 21st century. Most important, as traditional sources of funding have changed or declined, entrepreneurial public and private leaders are figuring out how to move their communities forward. Those leaders set their communities ahead of their peers and offer lessons for all. This publication highlights examples of urban and suburban leadership using innovative partnerships and financing.

Too often, cities budget all their resources for the challenges of today, such as crime and road repairs. They do not budget time and resources for tomorrow. If a community is going to succeed, it must invest in its future, whether that includes redeveloping vacant industrial properties, reinvigorating a declining downtown, or creating new employment opportunities by partnering with prospective employers.

Every community both large and small is buffeted by global and national economic forces. Those forces are relentless and will shape a community's future. For many years, the assumption has been that a local community's efforts can have little influence on its economic fortunes.

The narrative of communities being victims of forces beyond their control is true, but the assumption that communities can do little about it is untrue. Every community has a choice: to react and manage the effects of those global forces or to be proactive and decide what type of community it wants to be, based on its strengths. Every community has that choice.

A community's ability to change its trajectory begins with intentionality, the point at which a community decides to become something other than what it has been traditionally. Some of the great examples around the country should give every community reason to believe that local leadership can make a huge difference: the Research Triangle in North Carolina was an intentional decision to move from a tobacco and lumber economy to a technology economy; San Diego made an intentional decision to move from being just a military town to the fifth-largest technology economy in the country; Pittsburgh made an intentional decision to move from a failing manufacturing economy to a vibrant technology economy; Greenville made an intentional decision to revitalize its downtown by challenging the South Carolina Department of Transportation's rules for building roads and by creating a breathtaking linear urban park. Hundreds of other examples exist of communities that made intentional decisions to create a better future for themselves.

As a prerequisite for changing direction within a community, a clean, safe, and efficient governance structure is critical. **Communities need to be managed well.** The most obvious measures of effective management are the status of the streets and the local perceptions of safety. Clean, litter-free streets are an immediate indication that basic governance is working. Without a general sense of safety, nothing else works. To keep a community safe and clean requires a consistent, day-to-day focus with adequate resources and good management. Since public safety costs can represent 50 percent of a community's budget, the management of those resources is essential. The dollars must be sufficient to get the job done without being overbudgeted.

Once a community makes an intentional decision to change, a key set of ingredients must be in place:

- A clear understanding of a community's competitive advantages
- Strong leadership by both the public and private sides
- A strategic vision
- An entrepreneurial spirit
- A public/private partnership culture
- Knowledge of public financing tools
- A commitment to design excellence
- Organizational and staff capacity

Competitive Advantages

Communities must clearly understand their competitive advantages. Historically, communities were founded and grew because of location, available natural resources, transportation linkages, labor accessibility, or another unique characteristic or notable industry or resident. Often, the factors that shaped a community are either less important or completely irrelevant today. However, the legacy and talent generated by traditional industries can be the foundation of a new economy and can support creative financing for the community's future.

A clear understanding of the current strengths of a community will shape that community's vision. The vision must both encompass diverse opportunities for residents and nurture a rich sense of history, architecture, industry, culture and arts, institutions, and natural resources. **Developments happen incrementally, but great cities happen strategically.** The challenge is to use competitive advantages to fit pieces of the puzzle together to form a beautiful picture.

Leadership

Who is in charge? Most communities have invested in a vision plan, a comprehensive plan, a strategic vision, and other similar documents. Too often, those plans sit on a shelf because there are always reasons not to act, commonly because of community opposition. It is at that moment of doubt—when it is safer not to go forward—that bold leadership is essential. Communities that are succeeding have found the civic and political will to move forward with their vision.

Leadership comes from many places. Although, clearly, the most common model is the strong political leadership of a mayor, other models exist. In Cincinnati, one of this publication's case studies, the leadership came from the local business community. Executives faced a decision: either relocate their longtime downtown corporate headquarters because of declining appearance, poor building conditions, and increasing crime or assume the responsibility for reversing the trends. The business leadership created a development corporation—the Cincinnati Center City Development Corporation. 3CDC, as it is known, was seeded by the corporations with both multiyear operating funds and patient capital—equity funds not requiring short-term or full market-rate returns. 3CDC then partnered with the city's political leadership, created a focused strategic vision, and hired a great staff. The results are spectacular.

New Orleans's response after Hurricane Katrina is a great example of community-based leadership. Frustrated with waiting for mayoral leadership that never occurred, churches, nonprofits, individuals, philanthropic institutions, and a thousand other sources began rebuilding homes and neighborhoods and putting the pieces of a great city together again. Today, New Orleans stands as a powerful example of what community-based leadership can do. Unfortunately, a community-based leadership model rarely has the financial resources that are available to a strong mayor or business leadership group.

Several of the case studies showcase the role of local developers. Those local entrepreneurs joined with the city and started with an initial—often quite risky—project. Backed by a city subsidy and political will, they created a new reality. After the project succeeded, the market took note. Second and third projects took shape, and over several years—and focused leadership with strategic subsidies—the private market took hold.

A Strategic Vision

According to Joseph P. Riley Jr., longtime mayor of Charleston, South Carolina, "The best property in a community ought to be in the public realm." Waterfront trails, great parks, civic squares, and attractive shopping streets are examples of public properties that can satisfy Mayor Riley's vision for a community's best property. Developments are too often a series of transactions, disconnected from neighboring uses and those important public properties. A strategic vision connects transactions and views the initial public investments as catalytic. Such investments ignite interest and lead to additional investments that require fewer public resources.

The most vivid examples of a lack of strategic vision are the surface parking lots in almost every city, each serving individual buildings. Surface parking lots are the antithesis of a vibrant place. The ability of a community to manage individual property developers to collectively—rather than individually—solve parking, maintenance, design standards, and other common issues greatly affects the community's health.

An Entrepreneurial Spirit

At many different levels, a community must embrace an entrepreneurial spirit. The view "but that is how we have always done it" fails to support innovation that matches new technology and markets. Almost every community is being affected by demographic shifts as both baby boomers and millennials increasingly choose more urban, walkable living arrangements.

Communities need to rethink their zoning and parking regulations and to repurpose buildings that were originally constructed for obsolete uses. Those changes require rethinking the status quo. Often, community opposition to change stifles good ideas and inhibits progress. An appropriate and meaningful process for local input is essential, but the input process cannot be allowed to halt otherwise strong, new developments. Communities that succeed in capturing the opportunities in those new trends will be flexible, entrepreneurial, and open to public/private partnership.

A Public/Private Partnership Culture

Public/private partnerships are the most effective means to intervene in an uncertain or weak market. Partnerships share the financial risks between public and private entities. In addition to sharing financial risks, the public sector must often expedite approvals and streamline coordination among departments to move good projects along. Such partnerships require a clear understanding of the market conditions in the development area and a realistic assessment of the costs of infrastructure and amenities.

The use of public funds in private development is nearly always controversial. Yet, as the case studies that follow and hundreds of other examples show, the communities that invest in those strategic projects receive returns in recurring tax revenues, jobs, and the revitalization of often-distressed areas. The improvements within those areas are seldom achieved overnight. When focused and appropriate investments are targeted over years, entire communities are changed and become desirable places to live, do business, and invest in.

The most important positive impact public/private partnerships can have is catalyzing more development. In a healthy market, the development's return supports the associated costs; that is not the case in uncertain markets. But for public/private partnerships that use creative financing to underwrite the "gap" between market-driven development and higher-risk projects, the development would not move forward.

An Understanding of Public Finance Tools

Historically, federal urban renewal funds covered much of the public partnership in commercial and housing development. As those funds decreased, communities developed local tools, such as tax increment financing and tax abatement programs. Now, communities have become increasingly sophisticated in creating a menu of financing tools and layering them to make a development happen. Proper public subsidy can be tricky—not too much to line the developer's pocket unduly and yet sufficient to make the project feasible.

How often does one hear, "We would like to develop our downtown or revitalize a blighted neighborhood, but we just do not have the funds"? That viewpoint is an excuse to do nothing. As the case studies and financial tools section that follow illustrate, private and public funds are available and can be combined to create vibrant communities. There is some risk, but that risk is spread widely with a well-crafted partnership with the private sector and, most of all, a community vision.

Music Hall in Cincinnati's Washington Park has become a thriving entertainment mecca. *3CDC*

A Commitment to Design Excellence

Community welcoming signs frequently say, "We are a world-class community" or "a friendly community" or "a green community." No community's welcoming sign ever says, "We are a mediocre community." Yet the design choices a community makes for buildings, and particularly public spaces, are more informative than their signs, and they clearly identify "mediocre" communities. Great communities have great design. Charleston, South Carolina, recaptured its industrial and vacant waterfront for the public, building a stunning aquarium. Chicago built Millennium Park along Lake Michigan, providing diverse public spaces for both leisure and active uses.

In the past, communities were designed for automobiles: wide streets, often without sidewalks, and plenty of parking. People rebelled. Communities that are succeeding today have a unique sense of place built on history and nature. They are walkable and vibrant, with interesting architecture and a mixture of uses.

Organizational and Staff Capacity

Great developments happen because of a strategic vision and strong leadership, but at least equally important is a sophisticated and ethical staff. Putting together the details of multiple financing sources requires an organization that can respond to the initial proposal and can guide

A new generation of employment in the former Nabisco bakery in East Liberty.
ELDI

the development through the approval process. Whether a redevelopment authority, a local government department, consultants, or a private nonprofit entity, the lead organization and its staff must have both the responsibility and the authority to bring together money, land, and a sophisticated deal-making capacity.

Once a lead organization has been established, the supporting staff or consultants need the technical understanding of the many available federal, state, and local programs. That understanding is the *science* of the deal. The *art* of the deal is how creative advisers are in layering the various financial sources to make the plan work and to manage the partnership so that both the public and private participants succeed.

The intermingling of public and private funds for successful developments requires an absolute ethical framework. Nothing will destroy a community's ability to build productive public/private partnerships faster than questionable

deals. Generally, problems occur for two reasons: (a) a dubious relationship between the private developer and public officials or (b) uncertainty about the amount of funding and whether it is necessary. In successful partnerships, those two concerns will undoubtedly be raised, but the ethical actions of the partners can and must answer any questions.

Reaching for the Future

All too often, communities paralyze themselves because they do not believe that they have the resources to initiate change—and therefore they do not even try. This publication's case studies illustrate how communities have used and combined various sources of public funds to facilitate dramatic change. The Financing Transformational Projects section identifies the most common public programs and how they might be used. It also addresses the use of public financing to catalyze private investment in public/private partnerships, and projects the strengths and weaknesses of those partnerships. Finally, a checklist offers leaders, both public and private, an opportunity to analyze whether they are ready to move forward.

Every community has a choice. A community can choose to say it is "doing OK," or it can decide to enhance its standing by changing. That is a choice. This publication attempts to provide tools for community leaders to choose to reach for the future.

A team needs a common vision and a sophisticated understanding of financing.

Denver made a big choice, setting its future.

Fifteen years ago, with just two daily trains, Denver's Union Station and its 20 acres of little-used rail yards were a quiet place surrounded by exciting revitalization efforts on the 16th Street mall and the Lower Downtown district. In 2001, a partnership of the city and county of Denver, the state of Colorado, and the Denver Regional Council of Governments acquired Union Station and the property. In 2004, the voters of the eight-county Denver region approved a referendum increasing the sales tax by 0.4 percent to fund a 140-mile transit system with Union Station as the hub. The regional commuter system, known as FasTracks, and the revitalization of Union Station won a 2015 ULI Global Award for Excellence.

The complexity of the development required the creation of a unique management structure that brought together many public and private entities into an effective partnership. The coordination of the design, financing, development, and management was essential. The coordinating partnership became known as DUSPA, the Denver Union Station Project Authority. The membership included four government jurisdictions (city, county, state, and Denver Regional Council of Governments) and private members, including representatives from the Union Station Neighborhood Company, the organization formed as the master developer of the commercial, residential, and retail developments surrounding Union Station.

The design of Union Station and the transit hub is a remarkable success in integrating a complicated mix of often-unattractive transportation uses with open space and commercial, residential, and retail uses. The financing of the transportation infrastructure was also complex. DUSPA was able, first, to identify two sources of loans that would initially finance the development of the station restoration and, second, to identify revenue streams that would support the loans.

DUSPA identified two U.S. Department of Transportation programs that could be used for low-interest loans. They had never been used to support this type of commuter rail development, which added another roadblock. Sources of funds included the following:

Denver Union Station was brought back to life by the city of Denver and regional transportation agencies acting like entrepreneurs. *INFINITE_EYE/SHUTTERSTOCK*

- Federal Highway Administration, Transportation Infrastructure Finance and Innovation Act ($145 million)
- Federal Railroad Administration, Railroad Rehabilitation and Improvement Financing loan ($155 million)

The government entities along with a Special Metropolitan District provided tax increment financing and pledged the revenues to pay back the loans. In addition, DUSPA received almost $170 million in grants from 15 different sources, including both public and private funds, and $30 million from land sales to cover the $500 million costs of the restoration of Union Station, the development of the transit hub, other infrastructure improvements for the 20 acres, and parks.

The restoration of Union Station has catalyzed the most exciting new mixed-use development in the United States. Besides the opening of Union Station in 2014, to date there have been 2,100 units of new housing (apartments, condominiums, and affordable units) and 2 million square feet of office space added adjacent to Union Station, as well as striking new plazas and riverfront parks.

THE ART OF SIX DEALS

A S A COUNTRY, WE ARE FALLING IN LOVE with communities again. Whether in small towns, the suburbs, or big cities, the trends are on the upswing. Residential development is up; employment opportunities that connect to medical and university institutions are up substantially. Although the world is more connected technologically, the places that shout vitality and celebrate their authenticity are those where people want to be. Hundreds of stories are being written around the country of communities that are successfully creating great places.

Sugar Land is redeveloping the former Imperial Sugar Company site. *JOHNSON DEVELOPMENT COMPANY*

This publication focuses on six communities. Some are built on historic traditions, others are built on natural location, and others are newly built. Two neighborhoods are recovering from severe blight and disinvestment, two are suburban developments that have created a sense of place, and two are small cities that were watching their downtowns fail. In each case, to succeed required a strategic vision, leadership, and creative financing. The leadership rose in different ways but came together in effective public/private partnerships. In each case, the conversation started with "what do we want to be" rather than "how do we pay for it." In each case, the communities, each with a struggling economy, figured out how to finance their dreams.

That is the lesson: imagining a different future. Those six communities and the ingredients that were key to their success are:

▢ **East Liberty, Pittsburgh, Pennsylvania.** This Pittsburgh neighborhood is a lesson in *public/ private entrepreneurial culture*. East Liberty's revitalization was initiated by the public, built on by committed and savvy local developers, and repeatedly endorsed and supported by new public officials. A 20-year renaissance is still in the making.

▢ **City Center, Greenville, South Carolina.** A multiterm mayor and great staff held to a *strategic vision* for downtown, using public dollars and public spaces to reframe the city center. *Commitment to design excellence* transformed an eyesore road/ravine into a stunning pedestrian bridge with public walkways, creating a new urban center with first-class amenities.

▢ **Allentown, Pennsylvania.** Strong private leadership focused on the opportunity. Innovative state *funding tools* allowed state tax receipts to remain in downtown and to bankroll new construction of offices, a hotel, retail shops, and an arena. Strong local developers and business leadership were pivotal in embracing the new vision. Capitalizing on the city's *competitive advantages*, Allentown is enhancing the entire Lehigh Valley region.

▢ **Orland Park, Illinois.** In this Chicago suburb, the conversion of a classic suburban downtown to a modern mixed-use village was delayed by the recession. Public *leadership*, working with a citizen review board, stepped up its commitment—significantly increasing its financial risk—to realize the desired vision.

▢ **Over-the-Rhine, Cincinnati, Ohio.** Major local corporations knew how to lead change—and decided to reverse the decline of the downtown and a close-in neighborhood. Partnering with the city, a new, focused *organization* was created, which was privately funded for multiple years. A *sophisticated staff* was hired, and the truly staggering results are still underway.

▢ **Sugar Land, Texas.** Building on a rich history and an array of historic buildings, Sugar Land, a Houston suburb, used a *vision* and *strong design* sense to retool an obsolete manufacturing and processing plant as a mix of urban center uses.

EAST LIBERTY
A PITTSBURGH NEIGHBORHOOD

BECAUSE INVESTING POSED A HIGH RISK for private developers, local government played a pivotal role in early revitalization efforts. Located near downtown, East Liberty borders both a more affluent community and a lower-income community. A key first project, a home-improvement center brought residents together and kicked off two decades of revitalization. As the neighborhood transformed, perceptions of the market changed, and private developers gained the confidence to invest more heavily. The proportion of government subsidies declined, housing values rose dramatically, and crime fell by half.

East Liberty sits between the upper- and lower-income communities in the east end of Pittsburgh. *CITY OF PITTSBURGH*

Lessons Learned

- Initially, the city investment controlled a strategic site; then the city recruited a recognized, national tenant. That not only set the stage, but also sent a powerful message. The private market could gain momentum in the shadow of a national brand and continued public focus.
- Both developing and maintaining a partnership and a shared vision with local government, neighborhood organizations, developers, and financial institutions were essential to fulfilling the overall strategy in this multiyear success.
- Although the vision was clear, with public officials changing, communication had to be renewed continually and the dream kept alive as new actors on all fronts emerged.

The Setting

East Liberty is a bridge community, bordered on one side by several affluent neighborhoods and on the other by lower-income communities. Both markets were enhanced and came together through the vision of change. In the 1940s and 1950s, East Liberty was a thriving retail hub known as Pittsburgh's "second downtown." By the early 1990s, East Liberty was perceived as a less desirable community and was largely abandoned. The community still held potential, retaining a station on the Martin Luther King Jr. East Busway, a bus-only highway providing easy access to locations throughout Pittsburgh.

The Catalyst

In a city that had lost half its population, a decision was made to aggressively pursue new investment rather than manage decline. As a first step, early in the administration of newly elected Mayor Tom Murphy and with great controversy, the city shifted $6 million a year from the operating budget to cover debt service for a $60 million bond issue. Proceeds would be used both to acquire land and help finance catalytic developments. Over the next year, Pittsburgh acquired over 1,000 acres of vacant and blighted property across the city. The city empowered its Urban Redevelopment Authority (URA), led by Mulu Birru, to negotiate developments and manage the land and financing.

A national tenant built a high-quality urban store, jump-starting revitalization. *URA OF PITTSBURGH*

One of the parcels purchased was a vacant Sears building on 19 acres in East Liberty. The local neighborhood organization, East Liberty Development Inc. (ELDI), had long been working on a community plan with three primary goals:

- Restore community vitality and homeownership
- Improve retail and residential options within the community
- Capitalize on the location, bringing together higher- and lower-income communities, as well as offering amenities to adjoining areas of the University of Pittsburgh, Carnegie Mellon University, and downtown

The first project would set the tone. After acquiring the well-located vacant Sears site, long an eyesore, the city sought a tenant that would be widely recognized and draw shoppers from

> *"One of the advantages of the overall Choice Neighborhood is that it encompasses and builds on the momentum of the western edge of East Liberty—and brings that momentum and powerful positive impact into the adjacent Larimer neighborhood."*
>
> —Mindy Turbov, director,
> **Choice Neighborhoods,**
> **U.S. Department of Housing**
> **and Urban Development**

all community segments. The city spurred Home Depot to take a risk, invest its own equity, and open a market-competitive urban store. Home Depot opened in 2000 and became Pittsburgh's highest-volume outlet among its other area Home Depots. The company declared its long-term commitment to the neighborhood and created 250 jobs—employing many area residents who walked to work. As its part in the development, the city used a portion of the special bond investment fund it had created. Using a mix of those bond funds, other city capital funds, tax increment financing, and state of Pennsylvania funds, the city invested approximately 50 percent of the construction costs of the Home Depot.

Beyond Home Depot's immediate success, it had a larger effect on the community. Since the city was willing to contribute significant funds to help offset risk, other investors began to consider developing in East Liberty. A respected local developer, the Mosites Company, expressed interest in bringing in a Whole Foods Market. Whole Foods opened in 2002 on the site of an abandoned janitorial supply warehouse. The project cost more than $32 million, and public financing included $10.56 million in New Markets Tax Credit equity and a $1 million investment from various URA-administered funds, as well as state Enterprise Zone benefits. Whole Foods attracted a variety of patrons, including students from nearby universities and residents of both the Shadyside and East Liberty neighborhoods.

On the basis of sales volume per square foot, the Whole Foods corporate office designated the store as its "Rookie of the Year." The store created an additional 200 jobs. Following Whole Foods, Trader Joe's grocery opened in 2006. By leasing an existing space in East Liberty at market rent, Trader Joe's brought more food options to the community. With the commitment of three nationally recognized anchor tenants, the URA continued to fund projects that would fuel the community's revitalization.

Progressive Steps

The Mosites Company embarked on an adjoining 86,000-square-foot development that attracted Walgreens, FedEx Kinko's, Pennsylvania Wine and Spirits, Starbucks, and PetSmart. The URA also funded a pedestrian bridge, which served as a functional public art structure, further connecting Shadyside and East Liberty.

In 2007, Walnut Capital, a local residential and commercial development company, purchased an abandoned Nabisco property for $5.4 million and created a mixed-use development. Using a $1 million grant from the Pennsylvania Department of Environmental Protection, the contaminated building was remediated. The URA raised $10.5 million in tax increment funding, and in 2010 the former brownfield site was transformed into a $150 million mixed-use center called Bakery Square. The commercial space was leased to prominent local and national tenants, including Google. Bakery Square contains a total of 380,000 square feet of space, including a 120-room hotel, more than 1,000 parking spaces, and a new bus stop.

Bakery Square has received national recognition for its catalytic effect. Nearly 750 jobs were created, exceeding preconstruction estimates by more than 200 jobs. Undoubtedly influenced by Google's presence, the site housed one of the city's first locations for its new bike-share program, launched in 2014.

While Bakery Square was ramping up, community members sought a missing element: a general merchandise store. A 2011 development by Mosites met this need with a full-service Target that included a fresh grocery area. To ensure better public and private pedestrian access to the new developments, the city converted the outdated four-lane, one-way Penn Circle ring road to handle two-way traffic, with on-street parking. The road changes, which increased walkability, were warmly welcomed by management at the various commercial projects as well as by neighborhood residents.

In 2011, Walnut Capital continued its East Liberty investment by renovating a historic building into a luxury apartment complex, which quickly leased. From that project, Walnut gained a stronger sense of market conditions and the confidence to redevelop four smaller, vacant buildings into a $12 million, 85-unit luxury apartment complex with 16,000 square feet of retail space. As evidence of the strengthening market conditions, the URA was minimally involved in financing that development.

Bakery Square: before redevelopment, 100 years of Nabisco cookie smell gone. CITY OF PITTSBURGH

Bakery Square: after redevelopment. WALNUT CAPITAL

In 2013, Walnut Capital made an additional investment in East Liberty by purchasing from the city of Pittsburgh a 12-acre brownfield site that adjoins Bakery Square. In 2015, that second mixed-use development, known as Bakery Square 2.0, opened a 208,000-square-foot renovated office structure. A second office building of similar size recently broke ground, marking the first new construction in the area. Occupancy of the residential component of Bakery Square 2.0 began in June 2015 when the first residents moved into a 175-unit luxury rental building. Fifty-two for-sale townhouses are under construction, and another similarly sized apartment building was to open in June 2016. Bakery Square 2.0 is expected to create 1,200 new jobs as well as provide additional tax revenue. Estimates foresee the site generating income and sales tax revenues of $4 million, and total projected annual tax revenues of $7 million.

Simultaneously, Mosites began construction of a mixed-use transit-oriented development, East Liberty Transit Center. The six-acre project includes a reconstructed transit station, 3,000 square feet of commercial space, 365 mixed-income housing units with a large clubhouse, and approximately 570 parking spaces. Hoping to create a 24-hour neighborhood located right above the Pittsburgh busway, Mosites incorporated several outdoor spaces into the site's design, including a public plaza that links the development with the East Liberty Transit Center.

Recognizing the concerns regarding gentrification and the retention of a truly diverse community, the city worked hard to retain affordable housing. Three high-rise buildings, originally built by the U.S. Department of Housing and Urban Development (HUD) for low-income residents, were run-down and largely vacant by 2002. After lengthy negotiations, the URA convinced HUD to sell the blighted apartments back to the city

for redevelopment. The city carefully selected reputable developers committed to providing a well-managed and safe mixed-income community. Between 2002 and 2014, Community Builders Inc. and McCormack Baron Salazar developed $102 million worth of mixed-income housing, which provided 571 units throughout East Liberty.

Leadership

The East Liberty story epitomizes both public and private leadership. East Liberty Development Inc. created a neighborhood vision and advocated for investment. Mayor Murphy led the way in 1994, creating the city-backed bond fund and drawing in Home Depot. Local private developers like the Mosites Company and Walnut Capital joined with the city, took risks, and stuck with the development process through subsequent mayors, numerous changes to city council leadership, and neighborhood concerns. Developers were able to attract an array of national tenants, partially because the favorable financing allowed for early below-market rents in an attractive if unproven market.

Mosites and Walnut Capital were encouraged to do second and third projects after completing initial developments. The city worked to assist in financing projects, expediting the approvals process, and working with local neighborhood interests to accommodate a variety of legitimate needs for affordable housing and improved infrastructure and amenities.

Financing Mechanisms

Early East Liberty developments were heavily subsidized. By 2011, private developers were investing their own equity and using a variety of incentives, such as EB-5 Immigrant Investor Program funding, as well as loans from commercial banks. The market has improved sufficiently so that most public investments now cover extraordinary site costs, such as brownfield remediation and aging infrastructure rehabilitation. More than 20 funding sources—representing a total investment of $900 million—have been used to re-create East Liberty as a thriving community. Over the 20-year success in the making, the following sources have been used:

- New Markets Tax Credits
- U.S. Environmental Protection Agency brownfield funds
- HUD Section 108 financing
- Historic tax credits
- Transportation Investment Generating Economic Recovery (TIGER) grants
- Redevelopment bond issue grants and loans
- Land sales
- Tax increment financing
- Facade grants
- Bank loans

New housing has sprouted up in East Liberty. Above: Housing development followed the creation of a sense of place with added retail. *WALNUT CAPITAL* Right: When Google and other office development took place, new market-rate housing followed. *ELDI*

Return on Investment

Over the course of the past 20 years, over $900 million in new investment has come to East Liberty, adding over 2,400 new jobs. Almost 1,500 new housing units—at a variety of price points and in a variety of sizes and market configurations, from homeownership to affordable and luxury apartments—have been built or renovated. Two new hotels have opened. Over 400,000 square feet of office space has been developed. Both nationally recognized retailers as well as locally based restaurants and shops have found a home in East Liberty, restoring vitality to the community and making it a good place to both live and do business. The area now generates substantially more in city tax revenues, in addition to the new jobs.

CITY CENTER
GREENVILLE, SOUTH CAROLINA

COMMUNITY DATA

GREENVILLE POPULATION
100,000

GREENVILLE METRO AREA POPULATION
500,000

CHALLENGE
Declining downtown

STRATEGIC ELEMENTS
New road and pedestrian network
Linear parks
Public attractions
Market-rate residential
New hotel
New offices

GREENVILLE TOOK AN OPPORTUNITY to dramatically enhance its downtown area by opening up and preserving its waterfalls, creating pedestrian-focused places in the heart of the central business district. Residents and workers now use spaces that were once viewed as eyesores and unsafe.

Lessons Learned

- It takes time and persistence in the face of skeptics to make significant changes. Consistent leadership and focused attention are needed.
- Keeping an eye on the mix of uses requires good planning, not only at the beginning of the renewal, but also as the downtown evolves over the decades.
- Public investments should be catalytic and define the quality and excellence that are expected in private developments.

RiverPlace, a remarkable mixed-use development with hidden parking. *CITY OF GREENVILLE*

- Details matter. Downtown revitalization is more than big projects. All the "small projects" (landscaping, seating, lighting, and art) need to complement the overall vision.
- Developers must build for more than an eight-hour day. Jobs and business are keys to economic stability, but so are residents and visitors. A downtown must be a place with a constant critical mass of people. Art, cultural, and sports venues are an important part of that mix.
- More than capital must be contributed to the private development process. The public should be a reliable partner and should understand the components of managing a successful development project. The zoning and permitting process and design criteria are parts of the process that city officials can facilitate with little additional cost.

The Setting

Like many communities founded on a manufacturing economy, Greenville suffered from the manufacturing decline and experienced a severe decay of its downtown throughout the 1960s and 1970s. Residential and retail developments followed businesses out of the city in favor of suburban amenities. The downtown was left vacant and disadvantaged by a weak tax base. The city's leadership recognized that significant efforts must mitigate those changes and prevent further decline. Through city efforts with state officials and private business, a new vision for downtown emerged that would reestablish the city as an attractive place to be and that would create a viable business center. The community of Greenville is witnessing a revival of its central business district, at least 30 years in the making.

The Catalyst

A key part of the vision was the redesign of Main Street from a four-lane "throughway." Pedestrian-level interventions, attractive landscaping, and enhanced parks and plazas resulted in new narrow roadways. The downtown began to feel accessible and attractive in its own right, not as a throughway to elsewhere. The main streetscape plan was completed in 1979 and set the stage for public investment in strategic projects that have led to private sector year-on-year gains in the central business district. New offices, hotels, and residential developments continue to validate the strategy.

RiverPlace is just one of the wonderful examples of a successful public/private partnership in Greenville. As Economic Development Director Nancy Whitworth explains, RiverPlace is a "collection of buildings along the Reedy River with office buildings, residential condos, restaurants, artist studios, and an interactive water feature. This complicated public/private partnership required layers of ownership over different elevations." The developers had assembled ten acres over a ten-year time frame. RiverPlace is a $94.5 million investment with $27.5 million coming from the public through the use of tax increment financing, the local hospitality tax, and parking revenue.

Leadership

Since 1995, Mayor Knox White has served as a strong, guiding hand along with Whitworth.

Before redevelopment: a surface parking lot enjoyed the river view.
CITY OF GREENVILLE

Anchor projects that created and highlighted the natural, unique features of Greenville's downtown, developed through public/private partnerships, signaled to citizens and businesspeople alike that Greenville's public leaders were committed partners in the revitalization of downtown. Working with key stakeholders, the city steadily invested in key projects—Greenville Commons, the Peace Center for Performing Arts, West End Market, the Westin Poinsett Hotel, West End Baseball Stadium, and the pinnacle RiverPlace—that emphasized downtown Greenville's most spectacular feature, Falls Park.

As downtown began to rebound, a remnant of the original Main Street state highway was still blocking a 60-foot waterfall along the Reedy River, ignoring its natural beauty. In 2001, the mayor decided to remove the road bridge and "free the falls." Despite strong opposition, the bridge came down and was replaced with a spectacular 355-foot pedestrian suspension bridge. The road removal created the opportunity for 20 acres of linear parks and gardens. Today, families picnic, workers gather for their lunch break, and people stroll or run along miles of pathways. What had been a forgotten place has become Greenville's "Central Park."

Building on the success of the Main Street initiative, city leaders set out to establish a "business motive" for private enterprises and developers to consider downtown as an attractive investment option. City planning and investment used public/private partnerships to develop anchor projects that were indicative of the walkable community vision laid forth in the earlier plans.

With the demolition of the vehicular bridge over Reedy River Falls and the construction of the award-winning pedestrian bridge creating Falls Park, the investments in downtown Greenville accelerated. Developments such as RiverPlace, Project One, and EP360 include residential, commercial, and retail space; additional parking; and a striking river walk and public streetscape improvements. Approximately 75 percent of the investment in downtown Greenville has happened since the construction of Falls Park.

As trends for the office and residential markets move toward record levels of construction, rental rates, and economic return, the city is an outlier of downtown redevelopment considering its size. Thanks in no small part to the strategic planning of community officials and leaders more than 30 years ago, about 22.4 percent of the workers currently live downtown or within one mile of their jobs.

Financing Mechanisms

Since 1982, downtown Greenville has had almost $450 million in new investment, of which $123.8 million came from public sources and $325 million came from private sources. The public sources of financing included the following:

- Federal grants
- City general funds
- Tax increment financing
- City bond funds
- Hospitality tax funds
- Local parking tax funds
- Sewer and stormwater revenue bonds
- New Markets Tax Credits
- Land sales proceeds
- State and federal highway transportation funds

Managerial Highlights

From two of the key leaders in Greenville's renaissance, Whitworth and Downtown Development Manager Mary Douglas Neal Hirsch, come some managerial highlights over years of involvement in that transformation:

- Create a clean and safe environment. Nothing works if an area is not clean and safe. A consistent commitment of resources for maintenance is required.
- Provide signage, events, and food. Make it easy for people to find their way and give them many reasons to visit downtown. Attract great restaurants that have a variety of price points and offer different experiences, some with outdoor dining.
- Establish anchors. Anchors set the tone. Sports, culture, the arts, and great public spaces create vibrancy and need to be strategically located.
- Create a critical mass. Bringing people to live, work, and play is basic. Adding tourists creates an ever-changing mix.
- Become an entrepreneur. Both public and private partners need to be entrepreneurial—to recognize the inherent risks of development and be willing to assume risks and share them.
- Bring value to the private development. In addition to monetary support, the public can add value by expediting the approval process. City staff needs to be part of the strategic success team.
- Commit in writing. Make the partnership clear; stipulate the duties and obligations of each party.
- Include residential uses in downtown developments. Nationally, market trends are supporting walkable urban living. Success brings other challenges requiring a balance of residential developments with more traditional office and entertainment uses while maintaining affordability.
- Sustain public commitment and investment. Greenville's success is an example of visionary, effective, and persistent public policy. The long tenure of the mayor and key economic development staff members is evidence not only of success, but also of strong community communication over many years.

A visit to Greenville reveals the quality of the public spaces, the bridge, the streetscapes, the riverfront, and Falls Park to be consistently remarkable. The public and civic leadership that was required over 30 years is rare. In many ways,

After: a spectacular new park in downtown Greenville. CITY OF GREENVILLE

it is a model for other communities to learn how developments can happen strategically rather than as a series of disconnected transactions. Not by accident, each of the developments is of a consistent high quality. Clearly, a very effective public/private partnership philosophy has permitted Greenville to thrive as one of the best small cities in the United States.

Return on Investment

Over the period, property tax revenue has dramatically increased in downtown; it is now at $120 million and continues to grow. Hospitality and other economic development tax revenues have also grown steadily.

Although less easily measured, the attraction of downtown Greenville has been instrumental in both the city's and the region's economic development efforts. Downtown is truly a selling point when companies are considering Greenville. It is also crucial for recruiting talent: the vibrancy and variety of cultural amenities, entertainment, dining, and shopping in a great setting have made a difference. The national exposure—for example, *CBS This Morning* picked Greenville as one of the hottest vacation destinations—has drawn significant attention, and downtown is certainly the drawing card.

ALLENTOWN, PENNSYLVANIA
DOWNTOWN

ALLENTOWN WENT FROM A MULTIMILLION-DOLLAR city budget deficit to a multimillion-dollar surplus. It saw 4,000 new jobs come into the urban core and a billion dollars of new development. It is now the fastest-growing city in Pennsylvania.

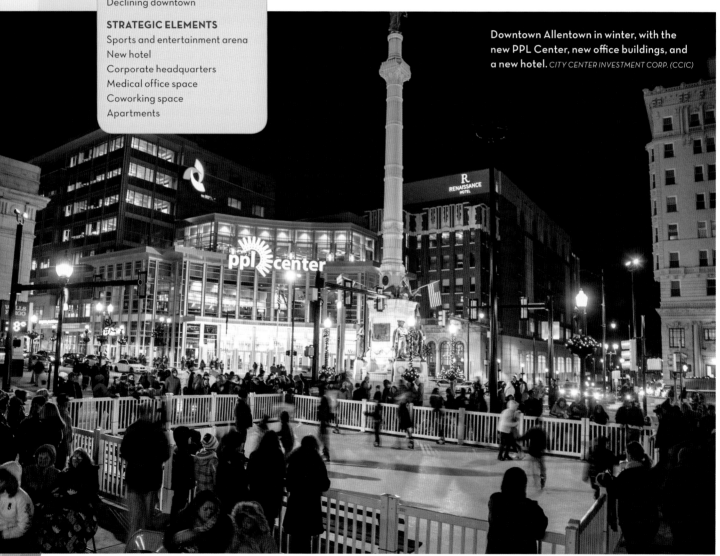

Downtown Allentown in winter, with the new PPL Center, new office buildings, and a new hotel. *CITY CENTER INVESTMENT CORP. (CCIC)*

Lessons Learned

- Recruiting bipartisan, committed advocates is essential to advancing state legislation that supports partnership investments greater than the capacity of local government.
- Designing incentives that increase as new buildings fill with employees and successful corporations will increase the vitality of the project area.
- Partnering with a strong local business community and committed developers can create the multiuse/mixed-use developments that draw beyond the project.

The Setting

Allentown is the most prominent city of the Lehigh Valley, which also includes Bethlehem and Easton. Although Pennsylvania's largest cities, Pittsburgh and Philadelphia, slowly revitalized over the past few decades, Allentown continued to decline. It took years for leaders to design and implement strategies to advance the Lehigh Valley as a whole.[1] The key was an innovative state funding program, a Neighborhood Improvement Zone (NIZ), and the vision of private developers who had faith in their hometown's economic vitality.

---

1   John Tierney, "Breathing Life into Allentown: Pennsylvania Comes to the Rescue," *Atlantic*, September 15, 2014, www.theatlantic.com/business/archive/2014/09/breathing-life-into-allentown-pennsylvania-comes-to-the-rescue/379742/.

Through the combined efforts of state legislators, the local business community, and local developers, plus focused attention, downtown Allentown is now a thriving mixed-use destination.

The Catalyst

The Pennsylvania legislature created NIZs in 2009. Through bipartisan and business support, the NIZ legislation was designed to use state resources to focus development and investment in Allentown. The NIZ designated a total of 128 acres—a significant part of downtown and a portion of the Allentown waterfront—as special taxing districts. By using tax increment financing, the NIZ allows revenues generated from local and state taxes (with the exception of school district and real estate taxes) to repay debt on bonds and loans that were originally used for capital improvements within the qualifying areas. A special entity, the Allentown Neighborhood Improvement Zone Development Authority (ANIZDA), was created as the conduit for the financing.

Tax revenues that typically would be directed to the state are instead redirected to Allentown for development. Figure 1 contains a list of those tax revenue sources.

Progressive Steps

New construction in the NIZ began with a publicly funded 10,000-seat arena, the PPL Center. The state-of-the-art sports and events arena is home

---

FIGURE 1. TAXES THAT QUALIFY UNDER THE NIZ

State taxes (Pennsylvania)		
	- Employer withholding tax	- Realty transfer tax
	- Sales, use, and hotel occupancy tax	- Title insurance
	- Corporate net income tax	- Company shares tax
	- Capital stock/foreign franchise tax	- Gross premiums tax
	- Malt beverage tax	- Gross receipts tax
	- Liquor tax	- Electric company
	- Taxes imposed on S corporation income	- Telecommunications company
	- Bank shares tax	- Transportation company
	- Cigarette use/excise tax	- Private bankers
	- Corporate loans tax	- Managed care organization
	- Public utility realty tax	- Net income tax—mutual thrift institutions

Local taxes (Allentown)	
	- Local employer wage/earned income tax
	- Local service tax
	- Business privilege tax
	- Licensing fee

Source: Allentown Neighborhood Improvement Zone Development Authority.

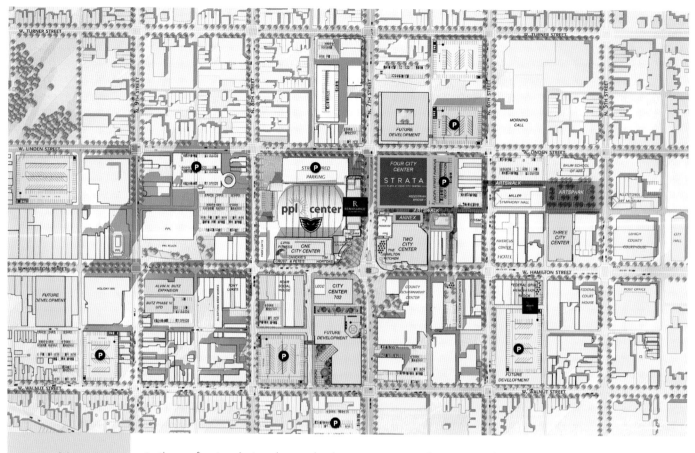

to the professional minor-league hockey team, the Lehigh Phantoms (affiliated with the NHL's Philadelphia Flyers). In addition to hockey games, the arena hosts a broad range of music and entertainment events throughout the year.

Next came a visionary private real estate development company, City Center Investment Corporation (CCIC), which relied on the NIZ as a financing tool in major projects to revitalize Allentown's downtown. Its NIZ-supported projects included the following:

- One City Center, a 187,000-square-foot Class A office/retail tower. Major tenants include
  - Lehigh Valley Health Network
  - A 170-room, full-service Marriott Renaissance hotel
- Two City Center, a 290,000-square-foot Class A office/retail tower. Major tenants include
  - National Penn Bank headquarters
  - Air Products
  - Dunne Manning Inc.
  - Starbucks
- Three City Center, a 166,000-square-foot Class A office/retail tower. Major tenants include
  - CrossAmerica Partners (previously Lehigh Gas)
  - Norris, McLaughlin & Marcus
  - Morgan Stanley
  - Alpha Graphics

FIGURE 2. ANIZDA FUNDS FLOW CHART

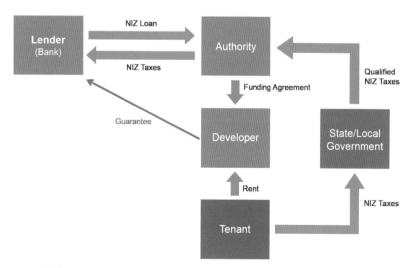

Source: ANIZDA.

- STRATA Flats at Four City Center, 170 market-rate apartments
- Velocity, City Center's coworking space located at 532 Hamilton Street, providing office space at below-market rates and networking opportunities to emerging and innovative businesses
- The Shops at City Center, 12 new shops and nine new restaurants
- Historic loft offices, first-floor retail space with creative loft-style office space above it

The initial success of One City Center was quickly followed by the construction of two additional office buildings along the main street with first-floor retail. Each of the buildings leased up quickly because of favorable rents, which were due to the NIZ subsidy.

The Shops at City Center and STRATA Flats are also fully leased, with plans for more residential development, attracting millennials and baby boomers alike. CCIC has also announced plans for its Five City Center Urban Innovation Campus, an entire block in Allentown that will include office, residential, retail, and green space—all designed to attract forward-thinking companies and their new generation of workers.

> "We went from a multimillion-dollar deficit to a multimillion-dollar surplus. We're seeing 4,000 new jobs come into the urban core and a billion dollars of new development."
> —Mayor Ed Pawlowski

Leadership

The city's success can be attributed mainly to outstanding public/private collaboration. That partnership's strength was fueled by the leaders' commitment to one common mission: to drastically improve Allentown. "We went from a

New life downtown on ArtsWalk. *CITY CENTER INVESTMENT CORP. (CCIC)*

Two City Center brings the National Penn Bank headquarters into downtown. *CITY CENTER INVESTMENT CORP. (CCIC)*

committed stakeholders to quickly move forward on initial projects, despite the many skeptics.

The Lehigh Valley region is unique because its leadership comprises members of varying political parties. The mayor, state senator, and private developers all eagerly pushed aside political partisanship barriers to revitalize Allentown. Those pragmatic public and private sector leaders worked together to prioritize economic development by investing in infrastructure, improving the region's quality of life, and helping train a versatile workforce.

Financing Mechanisms

In return for developing or renting in the NIZ district, several benefits accrue to participants:

- A 20 to 30 percent reduction in base market rental rates[2]
- Increased property values
- Public improvements to cleanliness and safety
- Increased sales traffic as revitalization occurs
- The ability to apply to the ANIZDA for future funding for additional projects

State Senator Patrick Browne explained that the NIZ legislation is not only repaying Allentown's debt on loans and bonds, but also breaking even and will soon be accretive for the state. NIZ tax returns are steadily increasing, allowing the state to be repaid. Under the NIZ structure, base NIZ tax revenues remain within the NIZ during buildout. Surplus tax revenues on each project then revert to the state. The state collected an additional $2 million in 2012, and

multimillion-dollar deficit to a multimillion-dollar surplus. We're seeing 4,000 new jobs come into the urban core and a billion dollars of new development," Mayor Ed Pawlowski explained. "We're now the fastest-growing city in the Commonwealth of Pennsylvania, and we haven't raised property taxes in nine years."

The founder and president of CCIC, J.B. Reilly, is an Allentown native and witnessed his hometown's decline firsthand. Reilly was inspired to invest further in the city and strategize ambitious plans for its rebirth. CCIC assembled a first-rate team of development, construction, and marketing professionals who worked closely with

2   City of Allentown, "Neighborhood Improvement Zone (NIZ)" web page, www.allentownpa.gov/Neighborhood-Improvement-Zone.

FIGURE 3. NIZ TAX REVENUE GENERATED AND USES, 2011–2014

YEAR	STATE TAX REVENUE REDIRECTED TO ANIZDA	USE
2011	$7.1 million	Half year, activity limited to land acquisition
2012	$30.9 million	First full year, construction gets underway
2013	$48.2 million	Construction ramps up, multiple projects underway
2014	$58.2 million	Arena and office buildings open

Source: Scott Kraus and Matt Assad, "Allentown Arena Zone Collects $48.2 Million in State Taxes: A City Construction Boom Brings a 56 Percent Increase over Last Year's Total," *Morning Call,* March 3, 2014, http://articles.mcall.com/2014-03-03/news/mc-allentown-arena-state-taxes-20140303_1_allentown-arena-zone-neighborhood-improvement-zone-anizda.

roughly $16 million in 2013 as new projects came on line, and about $18 million in 2014.

Figure 3 displays the total tax revenues generated and redistributed within the NIZ between 2011 and 2014.

Return on Investment

The downtown reached its goal of creating approximately 1,500 new jobs. As new businesses move into downtown, they bring more jobs with them. One of the attractive aspects of the downtown revitalization is that jobs range from entry level in the new Marriott hotel and retail outlets to professional and managerial jobs at Lehigh Valley Health Network, CrossAmerica Partners, and National Penn Bank.

Businesses from outside the region are now approaching Allentown officials and developers with interest in relocating to downtown. The improved ambience and infrastructure, and low cost of living, along with an array of new construction options, are drawing executives from New York and other higher-priced markets.

Although the crime rate in Allentown had already been declining since 2007, local residents are conveying a shift in perception. They credit an increase in pedestrian traffic, crowded restaurants, and stronger police presence in downtown for providing a renewed sense of safety. As a result, the city has been able to launch numerous cultural attractions, ranging from city art walks to concerts and sporting events. In 2014, Allentown was included in *Fortune* magazine's list of "Five Cities with Up-and-Coming Downtowns."

A view of downtown Allentown showing the new arena, office buildings, and hotel.
CITY CENTER INVESTMENT CORP. (CCIC)

New construction downtown spurred the restoration of historic buildings, attracting retail development.
CITY CENTER INVESTMENT CORP. (CCIC)

ORLAND PARK, ILLINOIS
A CHICAGO SUBURB

COMMUNITY DATA

ORLAND PARK POPULATION
60,000 located in suburban
western Chicago metro area

CHALLENGE
New downtown plans derailed by
economic recession

STRATEGIC ELEMENTS
Mixed-use destination with luxury
apartments
Medical office space
Lifestyle retail center

AFTER THE VILLAGE OF ORLAND PARK INVESTED $35 million in public infrastructure and land assembly, the real estate market collapsed and quashed anticipated development that would bring taxes to reimburse the village investment. When a new partner proposed a mixed-use project but could not obtain sufficient conventional financing, the village took the very risky step of providing a loan that completed the financial package.

New apartments offer more housing choices adjacent to the new transit station. *VILLAGE OF ORLAND PARK*

Lessons Learned

- The vetting of controversial projects will benefit from a citizen advisory board that thoroughly analyzes the project financing and works to answer any resident questions before the financial partnership recommendation is forwarded to elected officials.
- A concept plan is a "big picture" guide that must respond to market changes rather than precisely dictate development.
- A strong development agreement using well-researched market information suggests fair returns for both the private and public investment.

Achieving a future-serving vision often means overcoming significant obstacles created by forces that were not anticipated when plans were initiated. Both vocal opposition and difficult market conditions created numerous opportunities to derail Orland Park's village center project, an apartment complex with a commercial ground floor. Stable leadership and the methodical use of respected market advisers sustained the project.

Since 2010, four projects with more than $200 million invested have created a mixed-use, transit-oriented development. Orland Park has steadily implemented the live/work/play downtown envisioned in its planning history.

The Setting

Orland Park lies approximately 25 miles southwest of Chicago. Although many suburbs were created as bedroom communities and lack a sense of place and community spirit, Orland Park has successful shopping centers, a renowned school system, parks, golf courses, and a commuter train station with service to Chicago's Loop. A modest crossroads historic area is located near a new train station. However, that area did not meet the community's vision of a vibrant and defining downtown experience like that of several nearby communities.

In its comprehensive plan, approved in April 1991, Orland Park outlined its intent to create a "mixed-use site which includes government and recreation facilities, as well as office and commercial uses on a traditional village scale which reflects a small, compact development pattern." Although commercial developer interest in Orland Park was strong, it focused on the automobile-oriented opportunities associated with the community's regional mall rather than on the desired pedestrian-oriented village center.

Residential development increased Orland Park's population from slightly less than 40,000 in 1990 to 57,000 in 2010. The village recognized transit access as an important asset needing to be integrated into any new development. In 2000, a transit-oriented development (TOD) planning grant was awarded by the Illinois Regional Transportation Authority. As part of that planning effort, residential uses were added to the initial plan, which had constituted a purely commercial vision for the village center. The new TOD plan, completed in 2004, identified the need for new infrastructure—providing roads and municipal water and sewer service—as well as assembling correctly sized development parcels. Implementation of that plan continues today. Figure 4 diagrams the village center development context.

FIGURE 4. VILLAGE CENTER DEVELOPMENT CONTEXT

VILLAGE OF ORLAND PARK

Figure 5. Orland Park Village Center Plan, 2004–2008

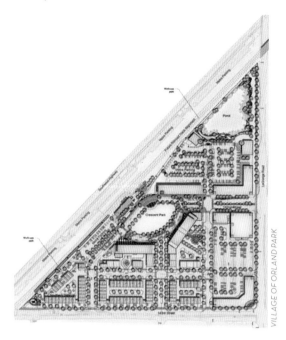

Expected Catalyst

Concurrent with the TOD planning effort, Orland Park established a tax increment financing district to fund the infrastructure that would ready the village center development. The village also issued a request for proposals in 2004 seeking a master developer to serve as an implementation partner. That partnership resulted in the plan illustrated in figure 5.

As part of the implementation efforts, the village obtained state funding to modernize its train station. The new station opened in 2007. Village center zoning was created to authorize the desired development. Backed by tax incre-

Since the success of Ninety7Fifty on the Park, construction has begun nearby on the park, the University of Chicago health center, and a CVS store.

ment projections, the village focused on acquiring property from willing sellers to assemble the village center parcels. Negotiations and marketing began, and a commercial developer simultaneously began constructing Orland Crossing on a nearby parcel. The lifestyle retail center component of that development, Development Area 1, was completed and largely occupied by 2007. The office and residential components composed a second phase to be developed, as demand was enhanced by the lifestyle retail center amenity.

In 2008, the real estate market crash ended private partner interest in both the village center triangle and the unfinished Orland Crossing. The village had invested more than $35 million in infrastructure and was condemning parcels needed for the transportation infrastructure. That predevelopment investment was expected to be recovered from the tax increment flowing from development. Without development, the village would be obligated to use other tax revenue to cover those costs.

Actual Catalyst

Recognizing that the altered real estate market was not reflected in the existing planning and marketing studies, the village commissioned new studies that revealed the need for a phased approach rather than implementation by a single master developer. That decision led to planning three separate parcels rather than a master plan for the whole site. Subsequently, a request for proposal for Development Area 2 was issued.

The selected response by Flaherty and Collins proposed luxury rental apartments, a parking garage shared by residents and commuters, and ground-floor retail and amenities. The respondent also recommended a smaller parcel. The approved development, Ninety7Fifty on the Park, began construction. The project consists of 295 residential units, 4,000 square feet of first-floor commercial space, 8,666 square feet of residential amenity space, and 365 on-site parking garage stalls situated on 3.4 acres of land. Occupancy began in spring 2013 and reached 93 percent in September 2014.

Since this catalyst project, the University of Chicago began constructing a four-

A train stop in the new downtown.
VILLAGE OF ORLAND PARK

story, 108,000-square-foot health center in Development Area 3. That development and an adjacent 530-space parking deck, which will serve commuters and the building, are on approximately two acres leased from the village. Orland Park officials estimate that the agreement with the University of Chicago will generate nearly $30 million in revenue for Orland Park over 25 years. Much of that will come from the land lease payments as well as sales tax revenue generated by both a CVS pharmacy on the ground level of the health center and a proposed restaurant north of the parking garage. Landownership will revert to the university after the lease agreement expires.

In October 2014, Chicago-based REVA Development Partners and Wanxiang America Real Estate Group broke ground on a 231-unit luxury rental community, the Residences of Orland Park Crossing. The first residents were expected to move in during summer 2016. This community is adjacent to the Orland Park Crossing lifestyle retail center and across the street from Orland Park's Main Street triangle development. It is a quick walk to the commuter train station as well as to shopping and dining venues at Orland Park Crossing. A new Mariano's Fresh Market opened in February 2016.

Leadership

The many changes and difficult market conditions created numerous opportunities to derail Orland Park's village center project. Leadership from Orland Park Mayor Dan McLaughlin, who had envisioned a downtown throughout his 20-year tenure, was critical to advancing the process. Economic development in Orland Park relies not only on its elected officials and staff but also on the advice of an appointed Economic Development Advisory Board (EDAB), comprising member bankers, real estate professionals, and local business leaders. The EDAB keeps the

Since 2010, four projects with more than $200 million invested have created a mixed-use, transit-oriented development.

focus on investment issues. It examines requests for village incentives and loans and then makes recommendations to the village board of trustees. It also reviews applications and development agreements before advising the village board on undertaking public/private financial partnerships. Its enabling legislation establishes a special focus on the village center and documents the criteria for public financial incentives. The EDAB thoroughly vets proposed financial partnerships and works to answer any questions before the package is forwarded to the village board of trustees.

At long last, Orland Park has the village center it sought.

Financing Mechanisms

Orland Park took the unusual step of financing the Ninety7Fifty on the Park project to bring it to market quickly. The goal was to add tax increment financing funds by capturing additional years of incremental property tax revenue. That additional revenue is needed to pay for the village center infrastructure. The village shared the development risk by designating the village incentive as a loan to be paid back only if the project's value exceeds the amount predicted when the redevelopment agreement was negotiated. Figure 6 summarizes the project funding.

Village funding involved a series of debt instruments used over the course of project implementation. Bond issues involved taxable general obligation bonds of $40 million and a line of credit that was converted to a term loan of approximately $22 million. Developer equity included a $1 million contribution and $1 million in deferred fees. In the very complicated redevelopment agreement, the developer loan was guaranteed, and the village loan essentially filled the "gap." It would be paid back only if the project outperformed the preconstruction estimates.

Although the redevelopment agreement anticipated that the project would reach stabilized rent of 90 percent in 24 to 36 months, that milestone was reached in only 18 months. Rents are also slightly higher than were anticipated during the project approval. Consequently, developer loan repayment began earlier than projected, and efforts are underway to determine how much of the village loan will be reimbursed from development profits above those projected during the redevelopment agreement negotiations.

For the University of Chicago medical center, the village provided a long-term land lease to lower initial developer costs. The medical center will make annual lease payments and pay property and sales taxes that cover the village's land costs. By sharing the cost of garage parking, this development provides spaces for commuters and residents attending evening events in the nearby parks and restaurants. Neither the developer nor the village alone could have justified the garage's cost.

FIGURE 6. CITY CENTER PROJECT FUNDING

Developer equity	$2,000,000
Developer loan	$38,234,707
Village loan	$25,000,000
Total	$65,234,707

Source: Village of Orland Park.

With a commitment to effective public/private partnerships, the village of Orland Park has to date brought together the following sources for financing its developments:

- Tax increment financing
- Federal and state railroad enhancement funds
- Ground leases
- Conventional bank loans
- Transit-oriented planning grants

Return on Investment

At long last, Orland Park has a viable village center with residential, office, retail, and parking.

Despite pitfalls and market setbacks, the project has achieved its initial goals and will repay the public investment in infrastructure funds and developer financing.

Orland Park has created jobs and led to the following new downtown investments:

- Lifestyle retail
- University of Chicago offices
- Public parking
- Housing units

The new village center integrates rental apartments and townhouses with shopping and nearby transit. *VILLAGE OF ORLAND PARK*

Over-the-Rhine Neighborhood
Cincinnati, Ohio

COMMUNITY DATA

OVER-THE-RHINE NEIGHBORHOOD POPULATION
7,000

CINCINNATI POPULATION
300,000

CINCINNATI METRO AREA POPULATION
2,100,000

CHALLENGE
Declining downtown neighborhood

STRATEGIC ELEMENTS
Historic building restorations
Revitalized parks
New entertainment, shopping, and dining
Condominiums
Apartments
Townhouses
Shelter beds
Parking

PRIVATE CORPORATIONS STEPPED UP to commit both major funds and needed leadership to a decaying neighborhood adjoining downtown. A new can-do organization was created, and a comprehensive, action-oriented strategy was developed that recognized the importance of the cultural amenities of downtown. Fountain Square, a Cincinnati landmark, was restored, and the neighborhood is alive with new housing and new jobs. By investing across the neighborhood—from homeless shelters to historic cultural amenities, as well as new housing, hotels, and offices—Over-the-Rhine became a national model of public/private leadership.

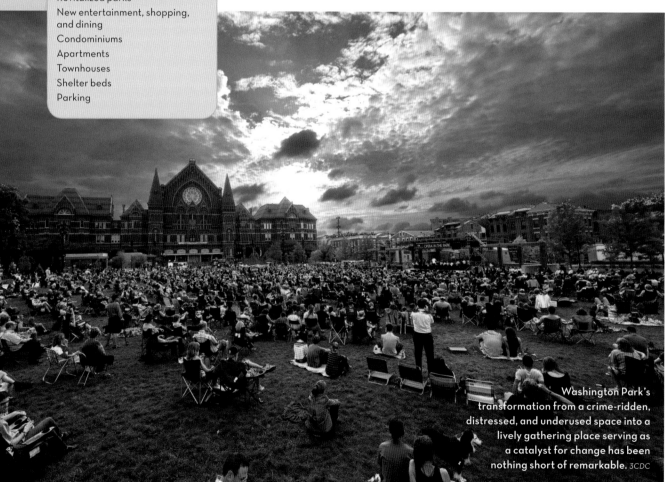

Washington Park's transformation from a crime-ridden, distressed, and underused space into a lively gathering place serving as a catalyst for change has been nothing short of remarkable. 3CDC

Lessons Learned

- Business leaders understood that without discipline, dedicated funds, and long-term focus and investment, the Over-the-Rhine community would not come back.
- A community-wide approach recognized the multiple dimensions of the neighborhood: from various housing needs to arts and cultural amenities.
- A dedicated, smart, and savvy staff that was able to work with the private business community, neighborhood leaders, and government entities made a huge difference. Those public/private practitioners bring a unique skill set and can be critical to success.
- Early land control and seed capital to fund the development corporation itself as well as initial projects were crucial. Secure multiyear funding by the corporations allowed for real strategic planning and implementation.

The Setting

Over-the-Rhine is a historic Cincinnati neighborhood adjoining downtown. Directly north of downtown, the neighborhood was settled by German immigrants in the mid-19th century and still contains splendid, largely intact 19th-century architecture and several good restaurants. However, decay was spreading, along with crime and disinvestment. Private corporations, led by Proctor & Gamble and Kroger, are headquartered in downtown Cincinnati, adjoining Over-the-Rhine. Dismayed by the deterioration, the companies decided to do something about the problems.

Over-the-Rhine's transformation into a vibrant Cincinnati neighborhood is a remarkable model for other communities in two respects: (a) the civic leadership demonstrated by the creation of a privately funded, nonprofit development corporation led by the business community, and (b) the array of creative financing and public/private partnerships, which were rapidly put together to accomplish the dramatic series of developments. The privately created nonprofit development corporation, Cincinnati Central City Development Corporation (3CDC) brought to Cincinnati what every community needs for its future: money, land control, and sophisticated deal-making capacity. The creation of the $50 million Cincinnati New Markets Fund allowed 3CDC to buy property

3CDC's mission and strategic focus are to strengthen the core assets of downtown Cincinnati by revitalizing and connecting the city's central business district (green) and Over-the-Rhine (red). *3CDC*

within an area defined by a strategic vision and to partner with developers who shared the same goals.

By aggressively acquiring over 1,000 parcels, 3CDC reached a threshold of development that gave people reason to believe the neighborhood was improving. The early restoration and enhancements in Washington Park and Fountain Square, highly visible public spaces, declared that downtown and Over-the-Rhine were coming back.

Every community can create a 3CDC-like organization. Too often, the response is, "We don't have corporate headquarters or big corporations like those that exist in Cincinnati." Every community has successful businesses and wealth from prior successes. Although the initial funding may be more modest, every community has the resources to create a private, nonprofit development corporation to invest in its future. By saying "We cannot create such a fund," communities are really saying "We do not have the leadership or commitment to our community's future."

The Catalyst

Like many midwestern cities in the mid-20th century, Cincinnati saw a decline in manufacturing, flight of the middle class from the city to the suburbs, and a resulting decline in the city center and downtown. Despite those signs of decline, downtown Cincinnati remained home to major

Before redevelopment on Vine Street: vacant and underused buildings, albeit nice architecture. *3CDC*

After redevelopment on Vine Street: in its 11-year history, 3CDC has restored 144 buildings, including housing and street-level commercial spaces. *3CDC*

corporate headquarters, including Proctor & Gamble, Kroger, and Federated Department Stores. Unlike many other cities where downtown housing was emerging to fill a market void, such housing was absent in Cincinnati. Downtown remained a nine-to-five environment, with streets virtually deserted when the workforce went home to the suburbs.

In 2001, a riot following a police shooting was a wake-up call. The slow decline of the central business district, the virtual abandonment of Fountain Square, and the extremely blighted conditions of the Over-the-Rhine neighborhood became the focus of civic and corporate leaders. The economic future of Cincinnati and the ability

of major corporations to attract the workforce they desired depended on a vibrant downtown.

In July 2003, the political, civic, and business leadership organized a private, nonprofit development corporation, 3CDC. Its mission was "to strengthen the core assets of downtown by revitalizing and connecting the Fountain Square District, the Central Business District and Over-the-Rhine." At that time, there were 500 vacant buildings and 700 vacant lots in Over-the-Rhine. Thirty corporate leaders make up 3CDC's board of directors; no public officials are members. Initially, 3CDC's operations were funded entirely by annual corporate contributions. Now, in addition to level annual corporate contributions similar to its initial funding, development fees and revenues from operating assets make up two-thirds of the annual operating budget of approximately $6 million.

The objectives of 3CDC are clearly defined:
- Create great civic spaces
- Create high-density, mixed-use developments
- Preserve historic structures and improve streetscapes
- Create diverse, mixed-income neighborhoods supported by local business

Early in 2004, the 3CDC board hired its first president/CEO, Stephen Leeper. Under his leadership, 3CDC began acquiring and land-banking blighted and troubled properties. Initially, 3CDC invested over $27 million in private funds to buy 200 buildings and 170 vacant parcels centered on Washington Park. Included in those purchases were several notorious bars and carryout liquor stores that were centers of crime and drug dealing. Later in the year, 3CDC leased and assumed management of the Fountain Square parking garage, which was municipally owned, deteriorating, and losing money, and began restoring the garage, fountain, and plaza.

Results

In its 11-year history, 3CDC has been involved in the following projects:
- Restoring 144 buildings, including housing and streetfront commercial establishments
- Constructing 50 new buildings
- Adding 1,113 housing units (condominiums, apartments, and townhouses)
- Providing 320 shelter beds

- Adding 156 hotel rooms
- Creating 845,000 square feet of commercial space
- Adding 2,700 parking spaces
- Revitalizing ten acres of parks, including Washington Park and Fountain Square
- Incentivizing millions of dollars in streetscape improvements

Financing Mechanisms

In addition to their private contributions for operations, 3CDC's founding corporations invested in a $50 million revolving loan fund, the Cincinnati New Markets Fund. In 2013, the board created a second Cincinnati New Markets Fund of $41 million capitalized largely by reinvestment of loans paid back from the first fund. Those funds offered patient loans as seed capital to begin and continue the revitalization of Fountain Square and Over-the-Rhine. The corporate leaders anticipated that the funds would be invested and leveraged in such a way that returns would be a possibility. The success of the first fund and the need to continue to reuse and roll over funds encouraged the second fund's investors.

With an entrepreneurial spirit and a commitment to effective public/private partnerships, 3CDC has to date brought together 17 sources for financing its developments.

As development took place, the perceptions of Fountain Square and Over-the-Rhine began to change. With 3CDC responsible for managing both Fountain Square and Washington Park, regular and frequent programming was offered, including music, food, and festivals. Thousands of

people who might have avoided the area are now discovering an interesting transformation. Over-the-Rhine and the central business district have become the places to go in the Cincinnati region for interesting dining.

Return on Investment

Since the creation of 3CDC, the change in downtown and Over-the-Rhine is nothing short of spectacular. Fountain Square and Washington Park have become "go-to" places instead of "go-from" places. A total of $842 million of new money has been invested in downtown and Over-the-Rhine, and over 2,500 jobs and 1,100 housing units have been created as a result. As part of the city's return, the downtown and nearby neighborhoods are now generating substantially higher annual tax revenues.

Over-the-Rhine: an up-and-coming entertainment and food district. Twenty-nine new restaurants have opened since 3CDC began its redevelopment work. J. MILES WOLF

City Gospel Mission is one of three new homeless shelters developed by 3CDC and its partners, yielding a total of 320 shelter beds. 3CDC

FIGURE 7. FINANCING

Total Investment: $842 million
Public funding sources
New Markets Tax Credits
Historic tax credits
Low-income housing tax credits
State New Markets Tax Credits
State historic tax credits
State low-income housing tax credits
State jobs funds
Unique private catalyst
Cincinnati New Markets Fund
($50 million revolving loan fund)

Sugar Land, Texas
Redevelopment of the Imperial Sugar Site

COMMUNITY DATA

SUGAR LAND POPULATION
83,000

HOUSTON METRO AREA POPULATION
6,200,000

CHALLENGE
Vacant historic factory

STRATEGIC ELEMENTS
City Hall
Hotel
Historic building restorations
Interpretive trail system
Sugar Land Heritage Museum
Performing arts center
Corporate headquarters
Condominiums
Parking

IKE MANY COMMUNITIES, the city of Sugar Land uses available municipal financing tools to enable successful development. But Sugar Land has expanded its concept of successful planned development beyond just the revenue stream and the typical public/private partnership. Its planned development efforts also incorporate the city's broader quality-of-life objectives, including the importance of cultural arts and preservation of the community's story.

Lessons Learned

■ Serving as a facilitator allows the city to be effective in its partnerships with developers while continuously educating the community. This approach consistently enhances local opportunities for successful planned developments.

Redeveloping the sweetest place in America. *JOHNSON DEVELOPMENT CORP.*

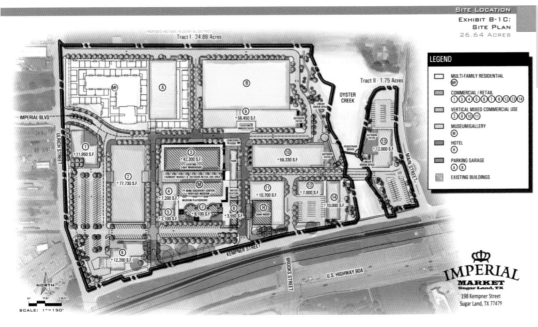

LEGEND

	MULTI-FAMILY RESIDENTIAL
	COMMERCIAL / RETAIL
	VERTICAL MIXED COMMERCIAL USE
	MUSEUM/GALLERY
	HOTEL
	PARKING GARAGE
	EXISTING BUILDINGS

Sugar Land's master planning efforts. *JOHNSON DEVELOPMENT CORP.*

A city hall and town square for a new community. *JOHNSON DEVELOPMENT CORP.*

- Incorporating historic and cultural resources into new development expands the opportunities for including new partners in the typical public/private partnership.
- Maintaining a focus on the city's mix of uses in planned development illustrates how those uses enhance the city as the best place to locate, whatever the reason.

The Setting

Sugar Land, Texas, is located just 20 miles southwest of Houston. As home of the Imperial Sugar Company for nearly 150 years, Sugar Land's name, heritage, and economy reflect its origins as a sugar plantation and company town. Imperial Sugar employed many residents, and company leaders supported Sugar Land and its institutions. Sugar Land was incorporated as a municipality in 1959 with a population of about 2,300. During the past three decades, the city has experienced rapid population growth, from slightly more than 8,800 residents in 1980 to about 83,000 in 2013. Sugar Land also increased in affluence and diversity and welcomed a large Asian population. Sugar Land has also grown through annexations and the development of a series of master-planned communities. The city's master plans and master-planning processes have been the framework for three significant developments over the past decade. Each development has unique financing attributes. Two of those develop-

ment processes are ongoing; all three exhibit the city's willingness to think creatively about development finance.

Sugar Land Town Square

Sugar Land's most notable and successful mixed-use planned development is Sugar Land Town Square. The first phase of that 32-acre, 1.4 million-square-foot mixed-use development was completed in 2003, with two subsequent phases. Completed in 2009, Sugar Land Town Square includes the town's City Hall with a 1.4-acre public plaza and event space, a 300-room Marriott hotel complex, three parking decks, 566,000 square feet of office space, 252,000 square feet of retail and restaurant space, and 167 condominiums. Sugar Land Town Square is located at U.S. Route 59 (I-69) and Texas Highway 6 in Sugar Land.

This development, originally conceived by the city in 1996, was designed to be Sugar Land's downtown, or central business district. The city passed the original planned development zoning specific to Town Square in 1998, with five subsequent modifications. Master developer Planned Community Developers Ltd. was engaged at that time. The project's financial challenge was to provide attractive lease rates for a project with high-end amenities and infrastructure. The city proposed Tax Increment Reinvestment Zone (TIRZ) No. 1 to enable reimbursement through public financing. This TIRZ process was protracted and took nearly three years to complete. Other taxing bodies participating in the TIRZ included Fort Bend County and Fort Bend County Levee District No. 2. The project ultimately required the city of Sugar Land to replace the local school district's participation in the TIRZ with the city's percentage of sales tax revenue generated by Town Square.

During this early phase of development, Sugar Land's city council had authorized the creation of the Sugar Land Town Square Development Authority to assist both the city and the developer with the Sugar Land Town Square development. Texas law allowed this authority to assist the city in its planning and finance functions. The city and developer had started discussions with Marriott to build a new hotel and conference center. The conference center required the city to finance its construction and the hotel's parking garage. The authority's focus became the development of the Marriott hotel and conference center with an accompanying parking facility in TIRZ No. 1. The development authority entered into a conference center and parking lease agreement with a private entity to lease and operate the conference center and to allocate parking garage spaces in Town Square.

One important city incentive tool that was applied during the development of Sugar Land Town Square predates its development. Sugar Land voters approved the creation of the Sugar Land Development Corporation in 1993. Organized

under Texas's 1979 Development Corporation Act, Sugar Land Development Corporation levies a 0.25 percent sales tax to fund incentives and infrastructure improvements that support economic development throughout the city. As of 2014, this fund had provided $68.1 million in capital improvements and $7.9 million in incentives specific to business recruitment and retention.

Town Square's second phase of development was initiated in 2005. The construction of the first Class A office building (with ground-level retail) in Sugar Land was key to this phase. With a $2.4 million incentive from Sugar Land Development Corporation, Planned Community Developers secured Minute Maid as its primary tenant, occupying 115,000 square feet. Minute Maid agreed to move its corporate headquarters to this Sugar Land location. As part of this incentive, Minute Maid, like all Town Square office tenants, was granted a seven-and-a-half-year 100 percent tax abatement for property improvements. This abatement is granted from the city and its TIRZ No. 1 partners, Fort Bend County and Fort Bend County Levee District No. 2.

Sugar Land Town Square has received multiple awards for innovative development over the years. Among them, *Houston Business Journal* recognized the development as its 2005 Best Community Impact award winner, and ULI Houston named Town Square as a 2011 Development of Distinction. TIRZ No. 1 property values have also grown exponentially. As of year-end 2014, the total appraised value of TIRZ No. 1 properties was nearly $96 million, up from a tax increment base of $5.6 million.

Imperial Refinery

Sugar Land's former Imperial Sugar refinery site, at U.S. Route 90 and Texas Highway 6, is another ongoing example of creative funding for redevelopment. In 2003, Imperial Sugar announced plans to vacate its 715-acre site in Sugar Land. The city approved a general plan for the site in 2007. An initial planned development application was submitted and withdrawn in 2008 because of the economic downturn.

The development structure for the Imperial Sugar site is complex. Cherokee Sugar Land LP and the Texas General Land Office own the real estate as tenants in common. Cherokee Sugar

Land Management LLC serves as manager of the Imperial Sugar redevelopment project. Johnson Development Corporation is the project's manager. The city has the following role within this structure:

- The city annexed what is known as Tract 3 within the overall Imperial Sugar redevelopment site. This tract, originally a state prison located outside Sugar Land's city limits, was formally annexed in 2005. Tract 3 and the former Imperial Sugar refinery form the 736-acre site included in the city's general development plan.

- Through the creation of the Imperial Redevelopment District in 2007, the district and its board implemented project plans for the TIRZ, considered a bond issuance, and established property tax rates for the district.

- TIRZ No. 3 was intended to fund infrastructure improvements for the Imperial Sugar site. The city and Fort Bend County are the participating taxing bodies. This TIRZ has an appointed board to review improvement requests. The plan for TIRZ No. 3 also includes funding for the preservation and reuse of former Imperial Sugar buildings, which are considered his-

toric locally, and for creating a Sugar Land Heritage Museum within one of those buildings. The city extended this TIRZ for an additional five years in 2013. The total estimated project costs to the TIRZ are approximately $147.8 million, including $4.7 million estimated for historic structures.

- The city contributed 0.5 percent of the incremental sales tax attributable to the Imperial Sugar development.

The original redevelopment agreement for the Imperial Sugar/Tract 3 planned development between the city and Cherokee Sugar Land LP was executed in 2007. One aspect of that agreement called for Cherokee to preserve the site's artifacts as public art and serve as the anchor for an interpretive trail system through the site. Plans were also made to preserve the char house and other significant Imperial Sugar structures, as "the historic focal point of the redevelopment."

This redevelopment plan was amended in 2010 to include parking and infrastructure for the construction of Constellation Field, Sugar Land's minor-league ballpark, and nearby commercial and residential development. It was amended again in 2014 to provide for major land use

The community is designed with plentiful green space.
JOHNSON DEVELOPMENT CORP.

Walking the new trails of Sugar Land.
JOHNSON DEVELOPMENT CORP.

changes: for 127 acres, originally proposed as office use, changed to single-family residential, and for 50 acres, changed from retail to office uses. Those changes altered the local real estate market.

This 2014 amendment to the development agreement had one unusual requirement—that the Johnson Development Corporation design and construct the infrastructure and office space in what is identified as Imperial Historic District 1 within two years. The historic district encompasses 45.8 acres. Within the identified Historic District 1, about 27 acres were included in the Imperial Market District final development plan in 2015. (Those various subarea plans conform to the general development agreement and amendments.) The overall goal for this project was to recognize the importance of this specific area of the city and its story.

The resulting Imperial Market District plan includes the preservation of four major and locally important buildings (char house, three-bay warehouse, engineering building, and container house), two silos, and two smokestacks, all constructed by Imperial Sugar during its time in Sugar Land. Construction in the Imperial Market District is scheduled for completion in 2017.

The three-bay warehouse will be reused as part of the district's nearly 270,000 square feet of retail space and will serve as the location for the Sugar Land Heritage Museum and the Fort Bend County Children's Warehouse. The char house is slated to become an Aloft hotel. The smokestacks will anchor a plaza near new commercial construction in the district, and the ground floors of the silos will be reused as restaurant space. In addition to the historic buildings and new commercial spaces, an additional 274 housing units and 86,000 square feet of upper-story offices are proposed for the Imperial Market District.

The Imperial Market District project has an estimated budget of $160 million. Johnson Development Corporation, as project manager, purchased the land in November 2014. The project will be financed with historic rehabilitation tax credits, funding through TIRZ No. 3, bank financing, and developer equity.

TIRZ No. 4

The city of Sugar Land created TIRZ No. 4 for a 30-year term in 2009. This TIRZ encompasses a 698-acre site at U.S. Route 59 (I-69) and University Boulevard, and the TIRZ's participating government units include two of Fort Bend County's municipal utility districts. The stated goal of this TIRZ is to support public improvements that foster employment, cultural arts, and entertainment venues within the district. The goal is to create a destination for activities.

This acreage was identified as a commercial development and is located adjacent to Telfair, one of Sugar Land's most successful master-planned residential communities. The developer for both areas is Newland Communities. The TIRZ acreage includes some of the last remaining sites for potential development along U.S. Route 59 (I-69). Major retail development, including Costco, is slated for those sites. Newland Communities and the city have actually partnered for the development of 300 acres, including a land exchange for a performing arts center. The city is financing the public improvements and facilities to support the objective.

Development to date at the site reflects the TIRZ objectives. Fluor Enterprises has purchased 50 acres for an estimated 750,000-square-foot headquarters building. Other medical and professional office space is planned for the site, and the University of Houston–Sugar Land has now located to the area. Sugar Land's new performing arts center, an $84 million, 6,400-seat theater, was under construction in 2016. The city has allocated $74.3 million in sales and hotel tax revenues for construction. In addition, the city has partnered with ACE Theatrical Group, which is contributing $10 million in equity as part of its 30-year contract to program the center. To sup-

port center operations, the city granted naming rights to Houston's Smart Financial Credit Union for $6.7 million. First-year projections put paid attendance at 26,000, with an annual economic impact of $26 million.

Sugar Land has used the availability of large sites and its location to use multiple financing tools:

- Tax increment redevelopment zones with other tax-participating units of government
- Nonprofit development corporations
- Sales tax contributions
- Hotel tax contributions
- Naming rights agreements
- Operator equity
- Historic preservation tax credits

A gathering at the Sugar Land public plaza. *JOHNSON DEVELOPMENT CORP.*

Financing Transformational Projects

CITIES, COUNTIES, AND STATES HAVE BECOME MORE CREATIVE in crafting development projects. As the case studies reveal, strong government leaders have successfully fostered entrepreneurship in the public sector. Local developers have stepped into that culture initially with one project and then continued their involvement through subsequent mayors and elected officials. If the initial project succeeds, developers often take on additional projects within a focused area, transforming a community or neighborhood. Various financing tools are layered to cover total development costs and required infrastructure. Even though such efforts take time and leadership, the results have been impressive and enduring.

Although the case study communities all used innovative partnerships and financing, they each started with a clear understanding of traditional real estate development finance and a goal of decreasing public interventions as markets gained momentum. The ultimate vision is market-rate development that attracts tenants or buyers willing to pay sufficient rents or purchase prices to provide a return higher or equal to alternative investments. In all of the case study projects, initial market conditions did not warrant new developments. Developers faced the choice of finding other locations or seeking a public/private financial partnership to fill the "gap" between expected returns and market returns. Creativity led to inventive sources of funds and committed tenants willing to take a risk that could lead to substantial returns.

Partnerships that equitably fill development gaps recognize both realistic development costs and appropriate returns on investment to both private and public partners. In the simplest partnership, the private investor's return on investment is either net income or a satisfactory sales price. The public's return on investment may include jobs, tax revenue, and increased private sector investment. Although both project costs and returns can be predicted during concept development, the uncertainty associated with those predictions in untested, pioneering projects adds

risk. Furthermore, difficult site conditions or a public vision that includes above-market construction materials or amenities can add to development costs. The project financing tools discussed in this section add layers of complexity to the simple investment model, but they are the financial basis for sharing the risks associated with transformational projects.

Financing Programs

The initial challenge for transformational projects is obtaining construction financing. As in market-rate projects, financing is composed of developer funds and various private loans. A public/private partnership adds government grants, incentives, and loans to the mix. All of the investor equity and government grants are at risk, whereas loans are secured by the project's assets. The loans are repaid at an agreed interest rate by a specific time and in a specific order. The equity investment is repaid only when the finished project is sold or if annual income exceeds expenses after completion. Governments may invest in the form of equity or debt, or most often "patient" debt—that is, debt that may have more liberal terms than conventional bank debt.

The information that follows highlights some of the government resources often used to finance transformational projects. This summary only hints at the financing options available to public and private partners committed to achieving transformation. State and federal agencies and elected officials should be engaged early to identify the full range of implementation funding available to specific projects.

Equity

Equity is increased by any government contributions to the project that are provided without expectation of reimbursement from the project's future income. Land provided for free or at below-market value and facade improvement grants are common examples of local government equity. Government programs that add equity to the financial package are very desirable because they reduce the funds that private investors must provide to secure conventional loans. When the government provides equity, conventional lenders may offer larger loans because the loan-to-value ratio is reduced.

Tax Credits

A tax credit is an amount of money that a taxpayer is able to subtract from the amount of tax owed to the government. Because developments often require several years before turning a profit triggering tax payments, tax credits are often sold early on to investors. Investors buy credits at a discount to the investors and can apply the full amount of the credit to their tax bill. Each state creates tax credit programs specific to its redevelopment objectives. The following are popular federal tax credit programs:

- **The New Markets Tax Credit Program was authorized to attract capital investment and direct it to low-income and underserved communities.** To qualify, a community must have a poverty rate of 20 percent or higher, or its median income must be lower than 80 percent of the statewide or metropolitan area median. The federal government administers the federal tax credits by allocating them through the Community Development Financial Institutions (CDFI) Fund. With this money, the administering entities are required to offer financing with nontraditional or more flexible terms than conventional financing, and the projects they select are, for the most part, those that are unable to qualify

FIGURE 8. NEW MARKETS TAX CREDIT PROGRAM: KEY TERMS AND RELATIONSHIPS

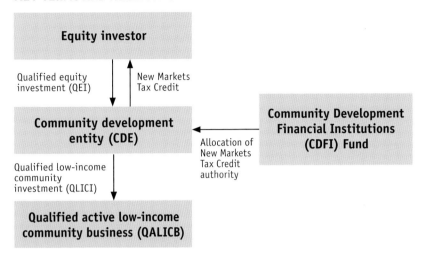

Source: Office of the Comptroller of the Currency, "New Markets Tax Credits: Unlocking Investment Potential," *Community Development Insights,* June 2013.

for conventional financing, or that could not qualify for enough financing to cover all of the project costs. In the case studies, 3CDC became a CDFI and then sold those credits to investors, thereby funding a portion of the desirable projects within the Over-the-Rhine neighborhood.

- The **Low-Income Housing Tax Credit (LIHTC) Program** encourages private investment in affordable rental housing for low-income communities. Successful investors will receive a credit equal to either 30 percent or 70 percent of the eligible project costs of low-income rental housing, depending on the type of credit offered. To be eligible under the LIHTC Program, developers are required to satisfy either the 40/60 test, where at least 40 percent of the units are set aside for renters earning no more than 60 percent of the area median income, or the 20/50 test, where at least 20 percent of units are set aside for renters earning 50 percent or less of the area median income. Investors receive the tax credits, and developers receive the invested dollars.

- **Federal historic rehabilitation tax credits** encourage the preservation of historic buildings by offering credit against federal taxes owed for renovation or rehabilitation. To qualify:
  - The property must be used for a business or other income-producing purpose.

FIGURE 9. TYPICAL LEGAL STRUCTURE FOR DIRECT INVESTMENT IN LIHTC-FINANCED PROJECT

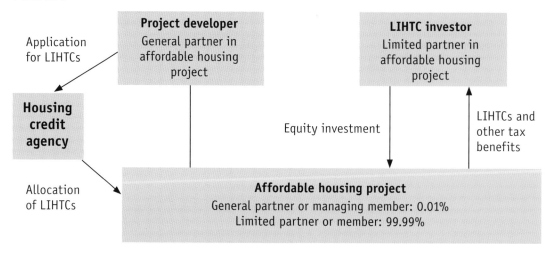

Source: Office of the Comptroller of the Currency, "Low-Income Housing Tax Credits: Affordable Housing Investment Opportunities for Banks," *Community Development Insights*, March 2014 (revised April 2014).

- A "substantial" amount must be spent on rehabilitating the historic building.
- The building must be certified as historic by the National Park Service.
- Rehabilitation work has to meet the secretary of the interior's Standards for Rehabilitation, as determined by the National Park Service.

Beneficiaries receive a 20 percent credit of the qualified rehabilitation expenditures for the costs incurred during the rehabilitation of a certified historic structure for commercial, agricultural, industrial, or residential rental purposes. A 10 percent tax credit of qualified rehabilitation expenditures is given for the costs incurred during the rehabilitation of an older, nonresidential structure built before 1936 that is not yet listed as a certified historic structure.

Community Development Block Grants

The U.S. Department of Housing and Urban Development (HUD) Community Development Block Grants (CDBGs) provide funding that can be used for urban redevelopment and community improvement. Entitlement communities—larger cities and urban counties—can apply and receive an allocation, and nonentitlement areas can apply for CDBG Small Cities Program funds. These grants are meant to help governments develop and

preserve affordable housing, provide services to vulnerable sections of the community, and generate jobs. Funds are allocated by HUD, then the local community is obligated to spend the monies per federal regulation on qualified projects.

Direct Municipal Investment

Any government funding that reduces developer costs can promote development by lessening the required project equity. Process incentives that speed development review can advance projects quickly and thereby reduce costs. Provision of free public land and government infrastructure investments, such as public streetscaping, public gathering spaces, road improvements, and parking, are examples of direct municipal investment that reduce project costs. The road and park improvements in the Greenville case study are good examples of well-used municipal investments.

Loans

When governments loan money for a transformational project, they help the project by providing those funds with more flexible terms. Such terms might include a lower interest rate, a slower repayment schedule, loan guarantees for funds borrowed from a private entity, or payment of a private loan's principal and interest for a certain period.

- **Revolving loan funds** offer fixed-rate and low-interest loans as a gap-financing tool for economic redevelopment projects. The fund is initially underwritten by public sources such as federal grants, state aid, or local funds, and private sources such as financial institutions or philanthropic contributions. Loan principal and interest repayments from project-generated revenues are recycled to finance future projects. The structure of loans, from interest rates to repayment methods, and the timing can be tailored to a specific project, offering more flexibility than commercial loans or debt financing. In many cases, revolving loan funds offer attractive but competitive interest rates: the flexibility with terms and collateral is the key benefit.

- The **Section 108 Loan Guarantee Program** is a component of the federal CDBG program. Under this program, banks and other financial institutions make loans and, if the borrower defaults on its loan repayments, the program compensates the lender. Section 108 guarantees financing for housing rehabilitation, public facilities, and large-scale development projects. Projects funded by the Section 108 Loan Guarantee Program must meet one of the CDBG's national objectives:
  - Principally benefit low- to middle-income people
  - Assist in the elimination or prevention of slum and blight conditions
  - Meet urgent community development needs that are of recent origin

- **Bond financing** offers long-term funding from state and local governments. Investors who purchase bonds are promised regular payments according to specified schedules. The extended bond repayment terms offer a quick source of cash to fund projects, generally paying only interest until the maturity of the bond. For large projects, the maturity can be up to 30 years, allowing plenty of time to complete the construction and earn enough money from project income and taxes to repay investors.

  There are two main types of government bonds. The first bond type funds "essential government functions" and must benefit the public. For these bonds, the interest paid to investors by the government is exempt from state and federal taxes. The second type of bond is a private activity bond. It is issued for the benefit of private individuals or entities

and is subject to state and federal taxes on the interest earned.

All bonds are subject to underwriting standards, which require a specific pledge of revenue to pay the bond's interest and principal. Redevelopment projects where the bonds will be sold in the market often involve tax increment financing backed by general obligation tax revenue. To ensure that the revenue actually covers the bond payments, there is often a provision that no more than 50 percent of the anticipated incremental revenue from a project can be dedicated to support bonds.

- **Land leases** are a development tool by which the public entity continues to own the land and rents its use to the development project. That feature allows the developer to avoid upfront land acquisition costs. Land rental payments may be subordinated to first mortgage interests, thereby further enhancing the equity in the project. The essence of the land lease is the government loan of the property for an agreed payment over time. That approach frees up cash for the developer for other uses and also improves the investment yield. Usually, land is leased for a relatively long period (50 to 99 years), but shorter leases can be structured to set the land purchase price on the basis of the development's tenants. Land leases also avoid the delay associated with negotiating a specific price for land. With a purchase price set in the future, the government can share in the project's success by setting the land price once the development is complete. **Land banks** are a tool to facilitate providing land for transformational projects.

EB-5 Program

The EB-5 Immigrant Investor Program gives visas to foreign investors who lend funds for projects that create at least ten American jobs. Although the basic investment threshold is $1 million, the minimum investment is reduced to $500,000 in targeted employment areas (TEAs). TEAs are designated as rural areas, or areas within a metropolitan statistical area that has experienced high unemployment. EB-5 funding is arranged

Figure 10. Basic TIF Model

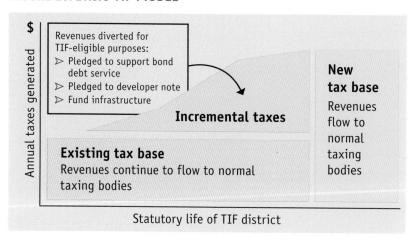

Source: Sarah Jo Peterson, "Tax Increment Financing: Tweaking TIF for the 21st Century," *Urban Land,* June 9, 2014, http://urbanland.uli.org/economy-markets-trends/tax-increment-financing-tweaking-tif-21st-century/. Inspired by graphics from the Council of Development Finance Agencies and Stephen Friedman.

through more than 700 for-profit "regional centers" that have government licenses to collaborate with private sector brokers that connect foreign investors with local projects. The review process for EB-5 projects takes approximately nine months, a significant delay compared with conventional bank financing. However, EB-5 debt may be considerably cheaper than conventional borrowing.

Revenue Capture

The government's confidence that the proposed project will exceed the private investors' expectations and generate new revenues for the government through taxes and fees is the framework for transformational projects. Loans and equity grants to public/private partnerships rely on sharing anticipated new revenues. A redevelopment agreement guides both the exchange of information on revenues and the distribution of revenues. The following information details programs that capture taxes that can fund local loans and grants as project incentives.

- **Tax increment financing (TIF)** is one of the most popular methods used to capture the annual return on investment from urban redevelopment. Although individual states vary in how they establish TIF districts and the allowable uses for TIF revenue, the TIF process is commonly initiated when a specific area is determined to meet the state designation

eligibility criteria. TIF operates by capturing incremental tax generated from the project developments. Several sources of tax revenues can be used to repay TIF bonds. Those sources may include property taxes; hospitality, convention, and arena taxes; rental car taxes; and so forth. Frequently, visitors and tourists are taxed, which is often more politically attractive than taxing local residents and businesses. As figure 10 illustrates, any additional revenue assessed after the designation date is segregated and will be used for projects within the TIF district. The amount captured is magnified when nearby properties increase in value because of an incentivized redevelopment. The anticipated new revenue from development can underwrite the issuance of bonds and can be applied to upfront project costs or can fund projects on a pay-as-you-go basis.

Although TIF is governed by state laws, implementation is a local decision, so municipal governments can exercise significant control and are not dependent on state or federal approval.

- **Tax abatements** return potential new revenue directly to property owners by reducing taxes or by exempting them from taxes for a specified period. Cities, counties, and states commonly grant tax abatements to incentivize development and job creation in underperforming areas. The reduced taxes cut expenses for the property owners and thereby increase their net operating income. They can be granted as

- A freeze on the assessed value of the property—any improvements to the site will not increase the taxable value of the property
- A tax reduction for a certain period (usually five to 25 years)
- An exemption from a portion of the assessed value

When the goal is to increase the number of stores and restaurants in an area, communities or states can implement **sales tax rebates**. These rebates encourage the developer to attract the highest-volume businesses to maximize the value of the incentive.

Income tax can be abated to encourage developers to maximize the number of employees in a project.

Business improvement districts (BIDs) are private sector initiatives whereby an area's businesses elect to self-impose a surcharge on their property tax to fund enhancement of the local environment. BIDs provide services that supplement those provided by a municipality, usually beautification, landscaping, marketing, and maintenance, security, and shared parking. Sharing those expenses reduces the individual property owner's costs and thereby increases the net operating income. Large, sophisticated BIDs can combine their assessment revenues with both private investment and state and federal grants to fund specific projects.

FINAL NOTES: LESSONS LEARNED

THE INTERMINGLING OF PUBLIC AND PRIVATE FUNDS for successful developments requires an absolute ethical framework. Nothing will destroy a community's ability to build productive public/private partnerships faster than questionable deals and relationships.

Generally, financing problems occur because of uncertainty about the amount and need for public funding. That challenge can be overcome by professional, independent review of projects and their financing. Sometimes such advice comes from local residents serving on an economic development commission. Advice can also be provided by consultants or staff members with extensive experience in reviewing financing packages. Communities engaged in the financing of development are acting as banks and must be as diligent as a financial institution in reviewing the credentials of proposers. The best predictor of a good outcome is previous, successful projects. Another indication of investor commitment is "skin in the game"—the amount of equity provided by the private sector.

1. **Choosing a bridge location and community "seam."** In the East Liberty and Over-the-Rhine areas, some definite distinctions existed between neighborhoods—one wealthier, one poorer, with some perceived or real barriers between them. By changing the land uses and building a bridge or common or shared spaces, the city helped both sides of the community gain strength, new retail and housing, and a stronger tax base and economy.

2. **Staying geographically focused with a goal/plan and strategy.** In each of the case studies, funders did not (and should not have) just subsidized every developer who walked through the door. There were geographic considerations, market strategies, and tenant adjacencies along corridor developments (such as along Hamilton Street in Allentown) that needed to be encouraged for good planning and enhanced market strength, regardless of ownership. Those are not programmatic subsidies per se—any historic building anywhere in the area can apply for historic credits—nor a proscription for catalytic community change. Low-income housing tax credits can be applied for anywhere in the city. The case study projects were catalytic because of the focus of resources: geographic, human, regulatory, and financial.

3. **Building on existing assets.** Identifying some strengths in the community can be part of the initial catalyst. Those strengths can be medical or educational institutions, active churches, or transit hubs. What already brings people to the area in a positive way? In East Liberty, the dedication of the neighborhood group East Liberty Development Inc. was significant in keeping the focus on the strategy and the accumulation of good projects over time. In Cincinnati, Washington Park and Fountain Square were critical public amenities to build upon. Greenville "freed the falls" and created an amenity that changed all of downtown.

4. **Moving to market: declining subsidy over time.** Initially, projects may require a public subsidy of 50 percent or more—from a variety of federal, state, and local sources. As success takes hold, public and nonprofit sources should be putting in fewer dollars, whereas the private marketplace is willing to put in more. That outcome should be a reflection of the declining risks and the greater faith in the marketplace.

5. **Establishing persistent focus and leadership.** In order to change a community, somebody has to pay attention. In several case studies, the mayor or government led the initial efforts. Local developers often took the first private risks. In East Liberty and Allentown, local developers worked with several subsequent mayors and public staffs and officials. In Over-the-Rhine, little happened until 3CDC got going and hired a dynamic executive director. In Allentown, the state representative initiated the creation of state financial incentive tools, but the real leadership came from the private developer City Center Investment Corporation, which has continued to buy land and concentrate money and effort.

6. **Cobbling together success.** Several of these stories illustrate the necessity of using many different financial tools and gathering various segments of the community to help. In Allentown, the museums and the arts community played a role; in Cincinnati, the commitment of the business leadership was essential to the revitalization of Fountain Square.

7. **Developing inclusivity: voices at the table.** Bringing the whole community together and into the improvements with the philosophy of everybody winning is important. However, that can be difficult and time-consuming, particularly in distressed and changing neighborhoods. In Sugar Land, historic preservation interests did not always agree with developers. For long-term success, all voices must be respectfully heard, including advocates for small businesses, affordable housing, and various age groups and lifestyles.

8. **Preparing for unintended consequences.** During the change process, both intended and unintended consequences must be addressed. Concerns about gentrification were considerable in Over-the-Rhine. In Greenville, the need for more or different infrastructure caused several years of downtown road construction and disruption. In Orland Park, the national recession derailed and stalled a good development. Broad-based and sustained leadership is critical to achieve community revitalization.

Whether as a public official, a businessperson, or a community advocate, people from all walks of life have changed the trajectory of their communities. The six communities portrayed in the case studies in this publication reversed their negative trends, employing a variety of tools to overcome the myriad challenges they faced. There will always be a hundred reasons why something cannot happen, and there is never enough funding. In each case study and in hundreds of communities across the country, the successes can be traced to an individual or a small group of people who were aspirational, who took risks, and who reached for the future.

Is it your turn to begin to write a new future for your community?

Are You Ready?

In the **Introduction,** eight ingredients were identified as keys to successful urban change:

- A clear understanding of a community's competitive advantages
- Leadership by both the public and private sides
- A strategic vision
- An entrepreneurial spirit
- A public/private partnership culture
- Knowledge of public financing tools
- A commitment to design excellence
- Organizational and staff capacity

The following checklist identifies actions that municipal leaders can take to establish a development environment according to these key ingredients. As you check off more items from the list, you are closer to positioning your community to achieve transformational projects as part of a healthy, vibrant community.

A clear understanding of community competitive advantages

YES	NO	
_____	_____	Do you know how you fit into the global economy?
_____	_____	Do you know how you fit into the regional economy?
_____	_____	Do the local government and the businesses and institutions driving the local economy have good relations?
		What are your big assets?
_____	_____	Surplus labor
_____	_____	Skilled workforce, such as high-tech employees
_____	_____	Favorable cost of living
_____	_____	Access to good transportation
_____	_____	Medical and educational research institutions
_____	_____	Tourist, historic, and entertainment destinations

Strong leadership

YES	NO	
_____	_____	Are local businesses and institutions active in community economic development organizations?
_____	_____	Can potential investors identify who is in charge of making transformation a reality?
_____	_____	Have the civic groups, businesses, and affected neighborhoods endorsed transformation?

A strategic vision

YES   NO

_____   _____   Are you clear on what kind of community you really want to be?

_____   _____   Is the geographic area clearly defined?

_____   _____   Is there passion for change?

_____   _____   Is a process in place for continuing the vision through political and economic change?

_____   _____   To let people know change is afoot, have the first key projects been identified?

An entrepreneurial spirit

YES   NO

_____   _____   Do vehicles exist to encourage and fund startups and entrepreneurs?

_____   _____   Is venture capital money available?

_____   _____   Is there a network of entrepreneurs to lend encouragement and support?

_____   _____   Do you have a business and resident community that supports innovation that matches new technology and markets?

_____   _____   If the risks are equalized to market risk, are there local developers who have the capacity, vision, and temperament to join with the public sector?

A public/private partnership culture

YES   NO

_____   _____   Are all potential partners, public and private, committed to transparency and a reasonable public process?

_____   _____   Are all partners committed to high ethical standards?

_____   _____   Are public benefits and goals shared, such as affordable housing and common amenities?

_____   _____   Is there sufficient time and patience to execute a complicated financial and approval process?

_____   _____   Is the desired project sufficiently important and catalytic that it is worthwhile for all parties to see it through to completion?

_____   _____   Can benefits be easily explained to everyone concerned, including the media and neighborhoods?

Knowledge of public financing tools

YES   NO

_____ _____ Do you have sufficient financial expertise to get the most out of the available resources? If not, do you have the budget to hire necessary skilled consultants or advisers?

_____ _____ Is your policy for determining financial incentives transparent and consistent?

_____ _____ Do the projected long-term financial benefits outweigh the near-term costs of financial incentives?

_____ _____ Are approval processes transparent and timely?

A commitment to design excellence

YES   NO

_____ _____ Do you have guidelines that clearly explain public design aspirations?

_____ _____ Do you know the difference in cost between standard design and the project requirements?

_____ _____ Have you identified entities willing to provide grants to support enhanced design?

_____ _____ Do you have a public art inclusion policy?

_____ _____ Do you have programs to maintain enhanced landscaping in public areas?

Organizational and staff capacity

YES   NO

_____ _____ Have you and your proposed partner(s) completed projects in this market?

_____ _____ In previous projects, did the proposed partner build what was promised?

_____ _____ Do you have employees or consultants who are qualified to review the partner's financial proposal and references?

_____ _____ Do you have written ethical reporting requirements?